HELPING ADULTS WITH
ASPERGER'S SYNDROME
Get & Stay HIRED

CAREER COACHING STRATEGIES FOR PROFESSIONALS AND PARENTS OF ADULTS ON THE AUTISM SPECTRUM

BARBARA BISSONNETTE

Jessica Kingsley *Publishers*
London and Philadelphia

List on p.46 is adapted from *Promoting Executive Function in the Classroom*, Meltzer 2010. Copyright Guilford Press. Adapted and reprinted with permission of The Guilford Press.

First published in 2015
by Jessica Kingsley Publishers
73 Collier Street
London N1 9BE, UK
and
400 Market Street, Suite 400
Philadelphia, PA 19106, USA

www.jkp.com

Library of Congress Cataloging in Publication Data
A CIP catalog record for this book is available from the Library of Congress

British Library Cataloguing in Publication Data
A CIP catalogue record for this book is available from the British Library

ISBN 978 1 84905 754 7
eISBN 978 1 78450 052 8

Printed and bound in Great Britain

"This coach___ ___ __ ___ __ ___ s with Asperger's Syndrome. Barbara does a wonderful job of sharing her experience and client's stories of applying for and getting hired for a job. The information she provides gives the reader very useful ways to approach the different steps of the employment process."

—*Mark Danaher, NCC, LPC, BCC, President,*
National Career Development Association

"What a fantastic resource for employers and professionals working with adults with AS! There is finally some growth of understanding and organizations for our adults, and this book is sure to become a universal reference, and a first read for students coming into the profession. Unfortunately being smart is not enough. Individuals with the designation of high-functioning continue to face significant employment challenges. Barbara Bissonnette's easy, understandable style and abundance of real life examples gives us the benefit of her extensive experience. It is material that I can use with my clients being concrete, realistic and detailed from each point of view."

—*Luby Aczel, Executive Director of The Specialists Guild*

"A remarkable book! Bissonnette lays out the latest thinking on Asperger employment and illuminates it with her personal insights and real world examples. She even corrects some of the bad advice others have been giving. It is a very practical, grounded approach. This is how autism employment needs to be done!"

—*Dr. Scott Standifer, author of* Adult Autism & Employment: A guide for vocational rehabilitation professionals, *founder of Autism Works Online and Director of Disability Policy & Studies, University of Missouri*

HELPING ADULTS WITH ASPERGER'S
SYNDROME GET & STAY HIRED

by the same author

**The Complete Guide to Getting a Job
for People with Asperger's Syndrome**
Find the Right Career and Get Hired
Barbara Bissonnette
ISBN 978 1 84905 921 3
eISBN 978 0 85700 692 9

Asperger's Syndrome Workplace Survival Guide
A Neurotypical's Secrets for Success
Barbara Bissonnette
Foreword by Yvona Fast
ISBN 978 1 84905 943 5
eISBN 978 0 85700 807 7

of related interest

How to Find Work that Works for People with Asperger Syndrome
**The Ultimate Guide for Getting People with Asperger Syndrome
into the Workplace (and keeping them there!)**
Gail Hawkins
ISBN 978 1 84310 151 2

Business for Aspies
42 Best Practices for Using Asperger Syndrome Traits at Work Successfully
Ashley Stanford
ISBN 978 1 84905 845 2
eISBN 978 0 85700 501 4

AutiPower! Successful Living and Working with an Autism Spectrum Disorder
Herman Jansen and Betty Rombout
ISBN 978 1 84905 437 9
eISBN 978 0 85700 869 5

An Asperger Leader's Guide to Entrepreneurship
Setting Up Your Own Business for Leaders with Autism Spectrum Disorder
Rosalind A. Bergemann
Foreword by Michael John Carley
ISBN 978 1 84905 509 3
eISBN 978 0 85700 978 4

With Appreciation

To my husband Michael for his thoughtful comments and suggestions about the content, and for his patience during the writing of this book.

To the many dedicated professionals who have shared their expertise and resources with me over the years.

To my clients for their talent and hard work, I wish you all every success.

CONTENTS

INTRODUCTION

MY PRACTICE AND PERSPECTIVE

My introduction to Asperger's Syndrome happened by accident. In the spring of 2006, I was finishing a graduate certificate in executive coaching at the Massachusetts School of Professional Psychology (MSPP). Four years earlier, I had quit my job as Vice President of Marketing and Sales at a publishing company. I was consulting part-time while exploring the career of professional coaching.

There is a saying in coaching that "sometimes your niche finds you." Like most who are new to the profession, finding the right client base was a process of trial and error. I was initially certified by the Institute for Professional Excellence in Coaching (iPEC) in 2003. I got my feet wet working with budding entrepreneurs and sole-proprietor business owners. My impetus for becoming a coach was a desire to give back my 20-odd years of business experience to people who could really benefit from it.

When I discovered that the MSPP was offering an executive coaching program, I eagerly applied. I set my sights on coaching executives in small- to mid-size businesses.

Thumbing through the MSPP continuing education catalog one day, I noticed a workshop about coaching people with Asperger's Syndrome. I had read snatches about Asperger's here and there, and it struck me as a very interesting subject. I gave myself permission to take a Friday off to attend the workshop.

That day, the fates seem to have intervened. Since the workshop started well after rush hour, I prepared to leave home without checking the traffic report. However, I suddenly felt compelled to go online and make sure my route would be clear.

Sure enough, the metro-Boston area was engulfed in an epic traffic jam. Nearly every major roadway was involved. Some people had been trapped in their cars for hours.

Ordinarily, I would have stayed home and avoided the 50-mile ride. But I *really* wanted to attend that workshop. Consulting a map, I found a circuitous route and arrived just in time for the start of the program.

I spent the better part of the next four hours literally on the edge of my seat. What I learned about Asperger's Syndrome was fascinating. The profile of social awkwardness sounded familiar. *I'll bet that I have worked with people who have Asperger's Syndrome.* A few weeks later, the executive director of the Asperger's Association of New England asked me a question that changed everything: "Have you thought about coaching people with Asperger's?"

I dove into the subject with what I imagine to be Aspergian-like fervor. I read every book I could get my hands on, attended workshops and conferences, and spoke to educators, advocates, psychotherapists and neuropsychologists. My idea of specializing in career development coaching for adults with Asperger's Syndrome was met with enthusiasm by every professional I contacted. "No one is doing that," they said. Finally, I had found a group of people who could benefit from my business experience.

Since 2006, I have coached hundreds of individuals with Asperger's Syndrome. My client base also includes people with Nonverbal Learning Disorder (NLD) and conditions like agenesis of the corpus callosum, hydrocephalus and attention deficit and hyperactivity disorder (ADHD). But most are those who know or suspect that they have Asperger's.

My clients range in age from 17 to 63. When I started, people came to my office in Massachusetts. Now, I have clients all over the United States, and even some in Canada and Europe, thanks to video conferencing via the Internet. This has given me a broad perspective on how Asperger's impacts employment.

People contact me for two reasons: they want to find the right job, or address performance problems at their current job.

In the past two years, I have worked with many more young people who are looking for work. They often have college degrees, some from prestigious universities. Still, they struggle to identify the right type of job, or don't know how to conduct a job search. Other job seekers are older and more experienced. They may have tried a variety of occupations without success. Although some have lost jobs due to layoff, most have not been able to meet productivity requirements, or adapt to change, such as having a new supervisor. They want to find work that is manageable.

Individuals who are employed have performance problems. These usually concern interpersonal communication, but might also involve productivity.

Their motivation to change is a poor performance review, disciplinary action or formal notice to improve. It might also be that the person is experiencing an enormous amount of stress trying to manage job tasks and get along with co-workers. He might want to discuss how to disclose Asperger's Syndrome to his employer, and request accommodations under the Americans with Disabilities Act (ADA).

Nearly all of my clients are in competitive, not sheltered or supported, employment. By this I mean they work in regular jobs that pay market wages. Some disclose their Asperger's Syndrome and others do not. A good percentage of them are in occupations that require a résumé and strong interviewing skills. (In Chapter 3, I discuss some innovative organizations that are providing supported employment that utilizes the intellect and unique abilities of Aspergians.)

A client might retain me to speak with his employer about ADA accommodations or other modifications that will enable him to be successful. A company may reimburse an employee for coaching services. Sometimes, organizations hire me to coach an employee. These engagements typically involve working with an employee who is a senior manager or director and his supervisor. A human resources manager is also involved. I do not provide on-site job coaching for the purpose of training new employees. This type of service is usually provided by non-profit or state vocational rehabilitation agencies.

Even though the majority of my clients would be described as "high-functioning" individuals, they face significant challenges finding and maintaining employment.

Maybe you are a parent or professional who supports an individual who requires greater assistance. There is much of value for you in this book. I coach people who struggle in entry-level jobs, as well as those who are in managerial or professional positions, earning over $100,000 per year. The same *patterns* are evident: difficulty interviewing, understanding employer expectations, interacting effectively with others and managing time and resources.

Aspergians are truly a heterogeneous population. Individuals vary quite widely in their abilities and need of support. There is no single approach or program that will address every person's needs. Strategies and supports must be chosen based on how Asperger's Syndrome impacts a particular individual.

Coaching provides individualized, one-on-one support that is beneficial to those who are able to follow through on assignments independently. On-site job coaching/training provided by vocational rehabilitation specialists serves those who need hands-on assistance. Supported employment enables those who cannot cope with competitive, open-market jobs to contribute and gain some measure of independence.

I also believe that greater employer education and involvement is required in order to achieve better employment outcomes. There is no doubt that the rates of unemployment and underemployment for individuals on the autism spectrum are high. Almost half of young adults with autism who are employed earn less than $7.25 per hour, and work fewer than 20 hours per week. In 2009, 33 percent of young adults with autism had jobs compared with 59 percent of all young adults with disabilities (Standifer 2011, p.5). I am not aware of research on the employment rate of individuals with Asperger's Syndrome, or the percentage who are working in jobs below their intellectual capabilities, but, clearly, those numbers are also high.

What is clear is that even the brightest and best-educated individuals struggle to function within the neurotypical workplace. It is ironic to me that we tell Aspergians that they need to be flexible, but how adaptable are we toward them? Currently, the expectation is that Aspergians will do all of the adjusting, in the very areas that are the most difficult for them.

On a positive note, my anecdotal evidence suggests that awareness of Asperger's Syndrome is finally making its way to the business world. This is due to the surge in individuals being diagnosed with an autism spectrum disorder. The Centers for Disease Control and Prevention estimates that 1 in 68 children in the United States has been identified as having autism (2014). Numbers this large are forcing parents, professionals and business leaders to be more focused and creative in finding ways to utilize autistic talent.

ASPERGER'S SYNDROME AND THE AUTISM SPECTRUM

Asperger's Syndrome was first recognized in 1944 by an Austrian physician named Hans Asperger. He wrote about a group of children with unusual characteristics including difficulty making friends, pedantic speech accented with odd vocal tones and rhythms, and consuming preoccupations with topics of special interest (Attwood 2007, p.11). Writing in his native German, Asperger's work remained largely unknown until 1991 when it was translated into English by a British researcher, Dr. Uta Frith.

Ironically, in 1943 Leo Kanner, an Austrian physician living in the United States, described individuals with what became known as "classic" or Kanner's autism. These severely impaired children were withdrawn, with limited or no language, and cognitive impairment (Attwood 2007, p.35). Both Asperger and Kanner used the word "autism," which is from the Greek autos, meaning "self." A British psychiatrist named Lorna Wing first used the term Asperger's Syndrome in 1981 to describe autistic individuals who did not match Kanner's description (Attwood 2007, p.35).

Autism was included as a diagnostic category in the third edition of the *Diagnostic and Statistical Manual of Mental Disorders* (DSM-III 1980). The DSM™ is used by clinicians to diagnose mental disorders. In 1994, Asperger's disorder [sic] appeared in the DSM-IV under the category of pervasive developmental disorder (Attwood 2007, p.36). It was considered to be a mild form of autism. Individuals who were diagnosed with Asperger's had no delays in language and no cognitive impairment.

Amid much controversy, the American Psychiatric Association eliminated Asperger's disorder from the fifth edition of the DSM, which was published in 2013. Asperger's and pervasive developmental disorder not otherwise specified (PDD-NOS) have been folded into the broad category of autism spectrum disorder (ASD).

In the DSM-5 autism is categorized as a neurodevelopmental disorder. The two basic diagnostic criteria are: deficits in communication and social interaction, and limited/repetitive behaviors or interests (American Psychiatric Association (APA) 2013, p.50). Some adults outgrow repetitive behaviors, and this has raised concerns that they would no longer be recognized as autistic under the new guidelines. However, according to the DSM-5, "Diagnostic criteria [for ASD] may be met when restricted, repetitive patterns of behavior, interests, or activities were clearly present during childhood or at some time in the past, even if the symptoms are no longer present" (APA 2013, p.54).

Social (pragmatic) communication is new to the DSM-5 and applies to individuals who have significant difficulty using verbal and nonverbal communication within a social context. It is differentiated from ASD by the absence of restricted and/or repetitive patterns of behavior, interests or activities (APA 2013, p.49).

Nonverbal Learning Disorder (NLD) is not included in the DSM. It is a learning disorder characterized by difficulty with nonverbal communication and pragmatics, deficits in visual-spatial processing and problems with psychomotor functioning (Thompson 1997, p.11). It is believed to be the result of damage to the right hemisphere of the brain (Thompson 1997, p.11).

About 25 percent of my clients have NLD. Some people believe that NLD is part of the autism spectrum, but I do not agree. Some of the symptoms overlap with autism, but they are not the same condition. For example, individuals with NLD are known to dislike change. However, their aversion is because of their weakness with visual-spatial processing (Thompson 2007, p.12). They have trouble making sense of and recalling what they see. Novel environments are avoided because of the amount of mental energy it takes them to orient themselves. This is different from the strict adherence to routine that is found in autism.

I notice a marked difference in the nature of communication problems between these clients. Individuals with NLD have intact theory of mind. They understand that people have thoughts that differ from their own. They may experience misunderstandings due to problems processing nonverbal cues, but they are able to understand why the conflicts or miscommunications occurred. Aspergians typically struggle to understand the perspective of other people.

Additionally, people with NLD are auditory learners. They talk themselves through situations, and ask lots (and lots) of questions. Individuals on the autism spectrum often have difficulty processing auditory information, and are visual learners.

Another key difference is the absence of restricted, repetitive patterns of behavior, interests or activities in individuals with NLD (Mamen 2007, p.80).

It is beyond the scope of this book to fully describe the differences between autism and NLD. Readers who would like to learn more are encouraged to consult *Understanding Nonverbal Learning Disabilities*, by Maggie Mamen (2007), and *Employment for Individuals with Asperger Syndrome or Non-Verbal Learning Disability*, edited by Yvona Fast (2004).

DO INDIVIDUALS STILL HAVE ASPERGER'S SYNDROME?

The changes to the DSM-5 provoked much dissension within the autism community. Some people believe that the changes are positive and others believe that they are not.

Supporters say that the single diagnostic category eliminates the ambiguity of differentiating between autism, PDD-NOS, high-functioning autism and Asperger's Syndrome. The diagnosis of an autism spectrum disorder is behavioral and based on the judgment of a clinician. Where indeed is the line between high-functioning autism and Asperger's Syndrome?

I count myself among the detractors. My concern is that the autism spectrum is so broad as to be impractical. At the "Kanner's end" are individuals who are nonverbal and have severe cognitive impairment. At the "Asperger's end" are people with doctoral degrees, who are married and raising families. Who is one referring to with the term *autism spectrum disorder*? The DSM-5 does offer three severity levels that clinicians can use: requiring support, requiring substantial support and requiring very substantial support (American Psychiatric Association 2013, p.52). Still, the range of impairment is enormous.

Another concern of mine is that most members of the general public—including business and human resources managers—know very little about the autism spectrum. Myths and stereotypes abound. Asperger's Syndrome is usually associated with an eccentric genius who works in high technology or engineering. Autism is linked to Dustin Hoffman's character in the movie *Rain Man*.

Employees who disclose a disability and request accommodations are almost always required to provide proof of a medical diagnosis. Dave is typical of my clients who work in corporations. "I'm afraid that if I told my employer that I have autism, it would ruin my career," he said.

Further complicating the matter is that Asperger's Syndrome is listed in the ICD-10. The *International Statistical Classification of Diseases and Related Health Problems* is published by the World Health Organization. At the time of writing, clinicians in the United States will be required to use ICD-10 diagnostic codes beginning in October, 2015 (American Medical Association 2014).

I faced a conundrum about how to refer to the clients I serve in the title and pages of this book. They are clearly high-functioning, and represent a small percentage of individuals on the autism spectrum. To avoid confusion, the publisher and I settled on the rather cumbersome term Asperger's Syndrome (Autism Spectrum Disorder).

I believe that Asperger's Syndrome will continue to be used informally to differentiate those on the Kanner's and Asperger's ends of the vast autism continuum.

WHO THIS BOOK IS FOR

I wrote this book with several audiences in mind.

The first audience is career counselors and coaches at colleges, universities and vocational schools, or those who are in private practice. The reality is that even the most academically gifted students with Asperger's Syndrome often struggle to identify occupations that are a match for their abilities. The information in this book will help you guide these students, and their parents, to degree or vocational programs that maximize the potential of gainful employment.

Vocational rehabilitation specialists, job developers, non-profit workers and other professionals will learn how to better assist job seekers, and then help them to maintain employment. Additionally, in Chapter 3 you will learn about some innovative organizations that are creating jobs that utilize autistic strengths. This book offers insight into the challenges that adults face, whether they are in entry-level jobs or corporate and professional positions. You will also learn about low- and no-cost accommodations that can enable individuals to successfully meet employer expectations.

If you are an employer or HR personnel, some of the client stories in this book will sound familiar. The material in Part I will increase your understanding of how individuals with Asperger's Syndrome process information. In addition to learning about their challenges, you will see how companies are tapping the talents of this educated and skilled labor pool. In Part II, you will find techniques for addressing common difficulties on the job.

Finally, this book is intended for parents and other family members of individuals with Asperger's Syndrome. In addition to practical ideas based on my experience of coaching hundreds of individuals, I believe that you will learn much from the experiences of others. The descriptions of social enterprises in Chapter 3 may spark an idea for a similar initiative in your community.

This book is not meant to be an exhaustive reference work on Asperger's Syndrome. My intention is to present an organized collection of "notes from the field," based on my experiences over the past eight years. My best learning has come from working with the men and women I have had the privilege to coach. The most meaningful compliments I receive are from Aspergians who say, "You really get it."

The book is organized into two parts and eight chapters. Part I is a primer on how individuals with Asperger's Syndrome think. The information may be familiar to parents, family members or professionals who work with this population, however, the many examples from my clients offer insight as to how the diagnostic criteria impact real people in the workplace.

Examples from coaching clients are found throughout this book. Some of these are in the form of client portraits, which offer detailed examples of how a particular aspect of Asperger's Syndrome affected a job seeker or employee. All names and identifying details have been changed, and, in many cases, composites have been used to protect my clients' identity and privacy.

Chapter 1 describes common workplace challenges that individuals experience in the areas of social interaction and communication, sensory processing and executive functioning. It also explains how over-reliance on routines, rigid thinking and fixating on areas of interest can interfere with making good occupational choices, and meeting expectations on the job.

The second chapter explores how problems understanding, expressing and managing emotions impact adults at work. It covers the ramifications of anxiety as well as the repercussions of impulsivity and inappropriate displays of anger or frustration.

Chapter 3 looks at how the strengths of individuals with Asperger's Syndrome can be utilized in the workplace. You will discover how several innovative organizations are creating employment opportunities to make use of autistic talents and abilities.

Part II of this book describes coaching strategies and how they can be applied to help individuals find the right occupation, and maintain employment.

Chapter 4 explains what coaching is, and how I adapt the coaching model for this population. You do not have to be a coach to use the techniques to assist students, job seekers and employees.

Finding the right job is the focus of Chapter 5. It covers the four factors that I believe are essential to occupational success for individuals with Asperger's Syndrome. I also explain why it is a mistake to base career decisions on interests alone, and offer specific suggestions for assessing abilities.

Chapter 6 is devoted to the job search. Individuals often become overwhelmed by the process of finding a job. I offer a wealth of suggestions for creating a realistic job search plan and preparing individuals for interviews.

There is a common saying in the Asperger's community that the real work for individuals is keeping a job. Chapter 7 covers the most common employment problems I see among individuals in my coaching practice. I offer specific tools that I have used successfully to help clients address communication and executive function problems.

Chapter 8 discusses the Americans with Disabilities Act, and how this law (and ones like it in other countries) protects Aspergians. Topics include reasonable accommodations, the pros and cons of disclosure at various stages of the employment cycle, and how to develop a disclosure strategy.

Finally, I conclude the book with some brief comments about what I see as a brighter future for many people with Asperger's Syndrome.

NOTE TO READERS

The word "he" is used throughout this book for consistency and to avoid gender-bias references.

Part I

A PRIMER ON HOW INDIVIDUALS WITH ASPERGER'S SYNDROME THINK

Chapter 1

COMMON WORKPLACE CHALLENGES

"I recently (4 hours, 37 minutes ago) found out that I have Asperger's Syndrome, and am interested in coaching to find the right job."

"I work well in quiet environments where I don't have to interact with strangers."

"My interests are writing, astronomy, crayons and looking at shiny things."

A few years ago, when I told people that I coached adults with Asperger's Syndrome, most gave me a quizzical look. Today, it is rare that I find someone who hasn't at least heard of Asperger's from a magazine article or television program.

While *awareness* of Asperger's Syndrome has grown tremendously, *understanding* of the autism spectrum has not. This is particularly true of adults in the workplace. Even at the time of writing in 2014, some people believe that: Aspergians are all geniuses who work in high technology or engineering; they are loners who do not like people; Asperger's is a personality problem; if you have Asperger's, you cannot make eye contact and have poor social skills (and presumably need etiquette lessons).

I believe that the key to understanding Asperger's Syndrome is to realize that it is a fundamental difference in the hardwiring of the brain. When I present a workshop or training to parents or professionals, I show the audience two photographs. One is of a small group of people conversing in an office. The other is a stylized string of the numerals zero and one, representing the binary code used to program computers.

I explain how neurotypicals naturally orient toward people. Our brains are hardwired to notice who is around us. For example, when I am in front of a group talking, I am very aware of the audience. I acknowledge attendees with a friendly smile. I monitor the emotional "pulse" of the room: Is the audience engaged? Are people taking notes? If the audience seems bored, I move on to another topic.

This is an example of the innate "social awareness" possessed by neurotypicals. Even when we are not consciously aware of it, we are adjusting our personal presentation and behavior to match what is expected in a particular situation.

Imagine that you are attending a professional training. You automatically know to wear business attire, not shorts and flip flops. Your conversations with other attendees will be about work, the program content or perhaps the lovely weather we're having. You will not discuss the fight you had with your spouse, or details about a medical condition. Your demeanor is different than when you are relaxing at home on the weekend.

These adjustments happen largely subconsciously. As a neurotypical, you do not need to expend mental energy to consciously think about how to behave at business gatherings.

Next I direct the audience's attention to the picture of the binary code. I explain how individuals on the autism spectrum naturally orient to facts and the physical environment. Entering a meeting room, an Aspergian might focus on an interesting pattern in the carpet, or begin counting the number of ceiling tiles. As he passes other attendees, his face is unsmiling, and his gaze is fixed on the floor or straight ahead. Should he see a familiar face across the room, he might spontaneously call out a friendly greeting, oblivious to the startled looks of others.

Once seated, the individual probably will not initiate a conversation, because he does not know what to say. Should a person seated next to him make a comment or query, he will probably respond with either two or three words, or an exhaustive monologue. The very proximity of strangers probably makes him very uncomfortable, and he unconsciously signals this with his stiff posture and anxious facial expression.

Continuing with my presentation, I stress to the audience that individuals with Asperger's Syndrome *want* to interact with other people. However, they don't know how. Since they do not possess the innate social awareness of neurotypicals, they must learn the rules of social interaction intellectually.

This is not easy. Imagine talking to your supervisor while thinking, *Look him in the eye, but not for too long or you'll be staring…his face just changed; is he upset about something? I can't tell…nod your head to show that you are listening…be careful what you say, so that you don't offend him like you did last time.*

It is nerve-wracking and exhausting for them to think through social interactions.

The official diagnostic criteria for an autism spectrum disorder include marked impairment in communication and reciprocal social interactions; and "restricted, repetitive patterns of behavior, interests or activities" (APA 2013, p.50). For the first time in the DSM-5 the presence of hypo- or hyper-sensitivity to various sensory stimuli (e.g. sounds, odors and tactile sensations) is part of the diagnosis.

Additionally, it is not uncommon for individuals to experience deficits in executive functioning, although this is not part of the diagnostic criteria. Executive function relates to the ability to plan, manage time and resources and solve problems.

Individuals with Asperger's Syndrome vary widely in their abilities, challenges and need of support. A person may not have all of the symptoms, or experience them to the same degree. For example, some appear awkward in their interactions with others, neglecting to make eye contact or to smile, or talking too loudly, softly or quickly. Others are charming and talkative, but may ask too many questions, or alienate others with odd behavior.

The following sections describe the primary challenges that adults face with social interaction and communication; adherence to routines and special interests; sensory processing and executive function.

SOCIAL INTERACTION AND COMMUNICATION

Difficulty with social interaction and communication impacts both job seekers and those who are employed. Hiring decisions are based on how well a person will "fit in" to an existing workplace culture. An employee who cannot function within a group faces limited career options and possibly multiple job losses— no matter how great his intellect.

Individuals with Asperger's Syndrome are commonly described as having "poor social skills." This implies poor etiquette. The deficits in interpersonal communication are much deeper than that.

Consider the typical banter between co-workers about a sporting event, popular television program or news item. Aspergians do not recognize such small talk as a means of building relationships. The exchanges seem silly, pointless and like a complete waste of time. A reader of my newsletter wrote to me with the following dilemma:

My co-workers tend to talk a lot about "girly" things like clothes and makeup, which I am not interested in. It is quite distracting, and makes it hard to concentrate on my work. How can I manage the noise levels?

It is quite telling that the reader wants help with the noise, not with finding a way to interact with her colleagues.

The reciprocal nature of social interactions is often hard for individuals to grasp. Aspergians communicate to exchange information. This often includes detailed facts about topics that interest them. There is usually little interest in seeking out information about others, and sharing emotional experiences. While a neurotypical might fondly remember the camaraderie of co-workers at a company outing, an Aspergian might recall what food was served and the activities that were available. Aspergians want to interact with others, and can form deep bonds. The *nature* of the interaction is different.

Newly hired at an information technology firm, 33-year-old Robert was determined to establish good relationships with his co-workers. He purchased a book about how to start conversations, and decided to try some of the techniques on a colleague during lunch. He was confused when his effort was not successful.

"What did you talk about? " I asked.

"Well, I asked my co-worker Dave how long he had been with the company," Robert answered. "Then I asked him where he went to school. Then I asked whether he was married. And then I asked where he lived."

After his last inquiry, Dave told Robert, "You ask way too many questions," and left the lunch room.

Robert had done an admirable job of showing interest in his colleague. However, by asking one unrelated question after another, the conversation turned into an interrogation. Robert did not intuitively understand that getting to know someone involves a back-and-forth exchange. He was surprised when I explained that he should also expect to be asked questions about himself by a conversational partner.

I coach clients who have worked with the same colleagues for years, but know nothing about them. These clients are branded "poor team players." They also miss out on important information that is not in the employee manual, like the boss's true priorities, who really makes decisions and using short cuts to increase productivity.

Even Aspergians who know the rules of social engagement have trouble applying them in real time.

I was struck by Eric's account of life inside a cubicle. The thought of a co-worker entering his space unannounced so unnerved him, he became hyper-vigilant to the sounds of footsteps in the hallway. Whenever someone approached, his hands would shake and his heart would begin to pound. Little wonder that by the end of the workday he was physically and emotionally drained.

No one will disagree that communication is a critical workplace skill. However, as my husband likes to remind me, it involves more than simply talking. Several complex skills are needed for the exchange of ideas, information, thoughts and feelings.

One of these is pragmatic ability. *Pragmatics* is the use of language within a social context (Fogel 2013, p.12). People with strong pragmatic ability base the content and style of their communication on the context of a situation, and the needs of listeners. They do not greet the CEO of the company with a casual, "Hey, what's up?" and a slap on the back. When an interviewer asks, "Who do you report to?" they say, "The director of marketing," not "Alice Johnson."

Pragmatic ability is dependent on correctly deciphering nonverbal signals. Almost all of what people communicate about their internal states comes from their facial expression, tone of voice, posture and gestures.

When I speak to groups I make this point by folding my arms across my chest, looking at the floor, and saying in a flat, monotone voice, "I'm very happy to be here talking to you about Asperger's Syndrome. Thank you so much for coming." Then I ask whether anyone in the audience believes what I said. On cue, everyone says, "No." They understand that the meaning of my message did not come from my words. It came from the way I *said* those words.

The well-known research of Dr. Albert Mehrabian revealed that only 7 percent of what people communicate about their feelings and attitudes comes from their words. Fully 38 percent comes from how the words are spoken, and 55 percent comes from their facial expression (Mehrabian 1981).

Individuals on the autism spectrum have reduced pragmatic ability. As a result, they take language literally and may not recognize metaphor, humor, sarcasm and implied meaning (Fein 2011, p.128). Twenty-eight-year-old Dean got himself into trouble by using expressions he didn't really understand. He told a family member that she had "obviously been around the block," thinking he was communicating that she was mature and sophisticated. He was aware of this problem and told me that he was determined to "nip it in the butt."

Aspergians frequently do not notice, or are unable to interpret, nonverbal cues. "How's that report coming?" a supervisor might ask in a strained voice, while looking at his watch. The Aspergian replies, "Fine," and continues with his work. Oblivious to the supervisor's distressed tone and attention to the time, he does not "hear" the real message: I am in a hurry and need you to work faster.

An individual may have little awareness of the nonverbal messages *he* is sending. How would you react to a co-worker who:

- walked directly to his cubicle without greeting anyone

- wore headphones for the *entire* workday

- stood silently outside your office while you were in a meeting

- shouted hello to a colleague at the other end of the hall?

After earning a master's degree in advanced mathematics, Adam was hired by an insurance company. He was confused by feedback from his supervisor that he needed to pay attention during staff meetings.

"I take notes of everything that people say," Adam explained.

Knowing Aspergians as I do, I had a hunch.

"Are you taking notes the entire time that you are in the meeting?" I asked.

It turned out that as soon as the meeting began, Adam started writing. His gaze remained fixed on his note pad the entire time. He was surprised to learn that this made it appear to others that he was not listening. Adam was relieved to know that there was a solution: look up from the notes at whoever is speaking to communicate that you are listening.

Job seekers with weak pragmatic ability may ramble during interviews, unaware that the interviewer is confused or wants to move on to a different topic. Those who speak in a monotone voice communicate a lack of enthusiasm or low energy. Individuals who show up weighed down with large tote bags, or portfolios crammed with dog-eared résumés or work samples, hardly project a confident, professional image.

Even *time* is a communication tool. A client may not know whether or not an interview went well. I ask how long it lasted. If he says, "about 10 minutes," I know that he is not being considered for the job.

The ability to make inferences about the mental state of other people is another critical communication skill (Fein 2011, p.105). Neurotypicals use various pieces of information about a situation to draw conclusions about how people are feeling, and what they are thinking (Frith 2003, p.77). This so-called "theory of mind" ability enables the recognition that people have thoughts, beliefs, feelings, intentions and desires that differ from our own (Attwood 2007, p.112). It is how we are able to understand and predict, with reasonable certainty, other people's behavior (Frith 2003, p.80).

Neurotypicals develop theory of mind ability automatically during childhood (Frith 2003, p.79). Individuals on the autism spectrum do not.

Several years ago, a client with Asperger's Syndrome, who lived in Boston, called to confirm directions to my office. "I'm going to rent a Zipcar and drive," Jeff explained.

"Okay. What's a Zipcar?" I asked.

"I can't believe you don't know what a Zipcar is," he said. He proceeded to describe a new service at that time that allowed people who lived in cities to rent automobiles by the hour.

When he arrived for his coaching session, Jeff reiterated his amazement that I wasn't familiar with Zipcars. "I can't believe you don't know that."

There was no judgment in Jeff's remark. He was genuinely perplexed that I did not know what he knew. Jeff didn't infer that since I drove my own vehicle to my suburban office, I might not be familiar with Zipcars.

Individuals on the autism spectrum have varying degrees of theory of mind ability.

Stephen was employed at a major corporation and started coaching to improve his presentation skills. His supervisor complained that he was far too detailed and didn't focus enough on strategy, particularly when meeting with the management team. We spent several weeks clarifying the needs of his colleagues in various parts of the organization. This was quite challenging for Stephen. How could he be expected to know what the managers in sales and marketing needed? Why wouldn't executives be interested in the fine points of how he performed his job?

Stephen thought in terms of projects, not the perspective of his audience. He struggled to determine what would be relevant to each group. On one occasion he exclaimed in frustration, "How can I possibly know what people want? Why can't I give them everything and let them decide?"

Another feature of autism that impacts interpersonal communication is a weak drive for central coherence. This is a reduced ability to comprehend the gist of a situation.

When Geoff was hired his supervisor told him, "If you have a question, just come and ask me."

A few weeks later, Geoff was completely surprised when, as instructed, he went to his supervisor's office and asked for help with an order. His manager said in a stern voice, "Not now Geoff, okay?"

Returning to his cubicle, Geoff was confused and angry. *I did what he said, and asked when I had a question*, he thought. *Now he's mad. What a nerve! I won't ask him for help again.*

Relating the incident to a co-worker, Geoff became even more confused.

"You didn't really go over and ask him that today, did you?" Geoff's colleague asked, incredulously.

The door to the boss's office had been closed for most of the past week. When it was open, Geoff and his co-workers could see tall stacks of papers on the boss's desk. If they ventured inside, the boss would acknowledge them by asking, "Yes?" without moving his gaze from his computer screen. On several evenings, as Geoff and the others were preparing to go home, they saw their boss paying for deliveries from the pizza shop.

Geoff's co-workers knew that their supervisor was tense and stressed as he prepared for the annual audit. They put his behavior into context: the closed door, stacks of paper, tense "yes?," take-out deliveries and the time of year. They all added up to Yearly Audit. Seen from this perspective, their boss's behavior made sense. The co-workers knew not to interrupt him unless the matter was urgent.

The co-workers had strong central coherence. They found meaning in events by putting them into context (Frith 2003, p.152). Autism researcher Uta Frith, who coined the term central coherence, explains:

> The normal operation of central coherence compels human beings to give priority to the understanding of meaning. Hence we can easily single out meaningful from meaningless material… Despite the processing effort that it involves, we remember the gist of a message, not the message verbatim. Furthermore, the gist is remembered better if it can be slotted into a larger context. (Frith 2003, p.160)

Geoff exhibited what Frith calls a weak drive for central coherence. He had "the unusual ability to disregard context" (2003, p.154) and missed the big picture. Taken out of context his boss's curt, "Not now Geoff, okay?" seemed contradictory and unfair.

The propensity to notice details and not the big picture means that Aspergians may miss the forest for the trees. Or, as Peter Vermeulen writes in *Autism as Context Blindness*, "Sometimes they do not even see the trees, but they do see the bark on the trees, the leaves, or even the veins on the leaves" (Vermeulen 2012, p.308). To see the big picture, a person must know which details are important, and this depends on situational context (Vermeulen 2012, pp.312, 314).

The weak drive for central coherence explains much of the difficulty that even very accomplished individuals have with communication. A person can understand the basic rules of communication, but unless he can quickly and accurately put interactions into the right context, he will not respond appropriately. It is not uncommon for my clients to realize how they should have responded after the fact, when they have had a chance to think a situation through.

Vermeulen suggests that individuals should be prompted about situational context (2012, p.309), when possible. Here is an example of how this works.

Amy didn't see the difference between preparing strategic responses to interview questions and lying. When asked at a recent interview about her weaknesses, she replied that she didn't like working with other people. "That's the truth," she said.

"I know it's true," I said, "but within the context of a job interview, it raises questions about your ability to get along with your co-workers. The purpose of an interview is to focus an employer's attention on your abilities."

We discussed why it was expected that job candidates would edit their responses in this way. Amy finally agreed that there could be several truthful answers to a question, and that some fit the context of an interview better.

HOW COMMUNICATION CHALLENGES IMPACT EMPLOYMENT

The intricacies of navigating the many and varied interactions that take place in the workplace cannot be underestimated. Take, for example, the simple act of greeting a co-worker.

Peter was eager to make the right impression on his colleagues.

"When I get into work," Peter began, "should I go to everyone's desk and say 'Good morning'?"

"No. You say 'Good morning' to the people you see in the hallway, on your way to your cubicle," I said. "If there are co-workers near your cubicle whom you are friendly with, you could stop by and say 'Good morning', if they're not on the telephone."

"If I say 'Good morning' to someone when I get into work," Peter wondered, "and then I see that person in the hall later on, should I say 'Good morning' again?"

"No, you wouldn't repeat 'Good morning'. But if you both noticed each other, you could acknowledge the person with a smile, or by saying, 'Hi,' or 'How's it going?'" I explained.

When he was finished writing down notes Peter asked, "What if my boss in the hall, and it's the first time I see him that day. Should I say 'Good morning'?"

These were legitimate questions from a man in his thirties who had earned a master's degree. This exchange illustrates how confusing interactions are for a person who lacks intuitive social understanding. For Peter, this simple act required conscious thought and planning.

For Terry, her supervisor's suggestion that she join her co-workers for lunch in the cafeteria was distressing. She usually ate a sandwich in her car. "Lunchtime is the only chance I get to relax all day," she said. "I don't have time to plan out what to say to people at lunch."

Pressed by her boss to "get to know people," Terry asked me to help her figure out what she could talk about with her colleagues. Like Peter, she wrote down notes so that she would remember what we discussed.

Poor social perspective taking can stall a job search.

Just three weeks after he started looking for work, Bruce was indignant and discouraged. "I can't believe that employers don't even have the decency to tell me whether I will get an interview," he exclaimed, his voice getting louder with each word.

"Most employers receive so many résumés over the Internet, they don't have time to respond to each one," I said. "They only contact people they want to interview."

"If that's how it is, then I'm not going to look for a job anymore!" Bruce sputtered, slapping his notebook.

Aspergian job seeker Justin was invited for a third round of interviews, unaware that this meant he was being seriously considered for the job. It annoyed him to be asked questions that he had answered during previous interviews. When someone he hadn't met before asked Justin to describe his strengths, he replied, "I have fully addressed that question three times already! The human resources, purchasing and office managers can tell you what I said." Needless to say, this ended Justin's candidacy.

Individuals vary considerably in their ability to interact and communicate with others. For some, the impairments are subtle and do not suggest that the person is on the autism spectrum. In some respects, this makes their situation more difficult because social gaffes are seen as willful, not due to a disability.

Common interpersonal communication challenges include:

- *literal interpretation of language:* an individual misunderstands job descriptions and interview questions, as well as employer expectations and feedback

- *reduced social filtering:* the person fails to adjust his communication based on situational context; blurts out the first thought that comes to mind; offends others with remarks that are too honest and direct; shares very personal information; dresses inappropriately or has poor hygiene

- *poor nonverbal communication:* makes inadequate eye contact or forgets to smile, and appears unfriendly, disinterested or dishonest; intimidates others by staring; looks angry when he isn't; communicates unease with unusual gestures or a closed body position; stands too close to others

- *doesn't engage with co-workers:* perceived as aloof, untrustworthy or unfriendly; becomes a target for bullying; is not privy to hidden workplace rules

- *interactions are one-sided:* frustrates others by only discussing topics of personal interest; dominates conversations; asks for help but never offers it; fails to learn about colleagues or their work; doesn't see how various tasks fit within the whole

- *interrupts:* communicates lack of interest in what others are saying

- *speaks in a manner that is too formal or pedantic:* appears condescending, arrogant or disrespectful

- *unusual vocal rhythm or tone:* difficult to understand; disrupts co-workers by speaking too loudly; monotone conveys low energy, confidence or enthusiasm

- *confusing narratives:* provides too little or too much detail; events told out of sequence; presumes that others share his perspective or understanding

- *misunderstands the motives, intentions and actions of other people:* unfairly blames or accuses others; reacts with anger or hurt to innocent actions; trusts those who are untrustworthy

- *inappropriate emotional reactions:* expresses levels of anger, anxiety or unhappiness that do not belong in workplace; individual is perceived as immature, mentally unstable or threatening.

ROUTINES, SPECIAL INTERESTS AND RIGIDITY

In addition to impaired social interaction and communication, the diagnostic criteria for autism spectrum disorder includes: "Restricted, repetitive patterns of behavior, interests, or activities," that may consist of, "inflexible adherence to routines," dislike of change, rigid thinking, and "highly restricted, fixated interests that are abnormal in intensity or focus" (APA 2013, p.50).

Clients have explained that certain habitual behaviors help them to manage stress. One man retreats to the rest room to flap his hands when he is feeling overwhelmed. After being around co-workers all day, a young woman needs time alone in her bedroom to gently rock back and forth.

As a rule, individuals on the autism spectrum do not like change and can become quite attached to routines. I believe that routines offer comfort in a world that seems random and confusing. This thought is echoed by best-selling author and Aspergian David Finch in *The Journal of Best Practices, A Memoir of Marriage, Asperger Syndrome, and One Man's Quest to Be a Better Husband.* He writes:

> I felt an unusual sense of peace as I prepared for my evening routine. At eight thirty each night, after the kids have been put to bed, I circle the first floor, counterclockwise, starting in the kitchen, where I check to see if the patio door is locked. Then it's back to the kitchen, where I usually wander around in circles…
>
> I proceeded through the dining room and living room, then it was on to the foyer, where I always take a few moments to stare out the front window, visually lining up the neighbors' rooftops (the alignment is the same every time, which is so gratifying it makes my shoulders relax, and for a moment my head is clear, my thoughts organized). (Finch 2012, pp.2, 3)

It can be quite unsettling when routines are interrupted. An attendee at one of my workshops apologized for leaving early. "I enjoyed your presentation and learned a lot," she said, "but had to leave before the end because I eat dinner at 7:30."

Individuals may resist change, even when their current situation is causing great stress.

Theresa was barely managing the demands of her administrative position. Her employer offered her a less taxing job at a regional office that was nearer to her home. Theresa agreed that it was a better fit. However, she decided to turn it down.

I summarized the negative aspects of her current job: the strained relationship with her boss, too much multitasking, a long commute and her dislike of the physical office. Then I listed all of the positives associated with the new position.

"I'm surprised," I said, "that you don't want to accept the new job. You are currently on formal notice to improve, and you have repeatedly said that you cannot manage all of your assigned tasks."

"You're right," Theresa said, and paused for a few seconds. "The other job would be much better. The problem is, I just don't like change."

Theresa was anxious about learning new tasks, interacting with new co-workers, adjusting her work hours and travelling to a different office. Eventually, she did decide to accept the new job and told me that she was doing well.

The term "restricted" refers to interests that are limited in some way. For example, an autistic child who receives a toy car might focus on certain parts rather than the object as a whole. Instead of "driving" the automobile on an adventure, he simply spins one of its wheels.

In an adult, restricted interest in an occupation may result in an inaccurate picture of what a job really involves. Denise wanted to be a nurse. When I asked why she was interested in this occupation she said, "I want to help people." However, Denise was explicit in stating that she wanted minimal interaction with others during the workday. She did not see the conflict until I pointed it out. (For more on restricted interests and career choice, see Chapter 5.)

Special interests ("fixated interests" in DSM parlance) are common among many, but not all, Aspergians. These are distinctly different than hobbies. Special interests are pursued with an intensity that can border on obsession. Even very young children can develop encyclopedic knowledge about their chosen topic, which might be quite unusual (think washing machines or steam engines). Individuals report that engaging in their special interest is enjoyable and relaxing.

The story of Michael Burry is a fascinating example of how a special interest can lead to a career. Burry is a physician-turned-hedge-fund-manager with Asperger's Syndrome. He was featured in *The Big Short: Inside the Doomsday Machine*, an account of the 2007 financial crisis written by Michael Lewis.

In 2004, Burry became intensely interested in the bond market. "He learned all he could about how money got borrowed and lent in America. He didn't talk to anyone about what became his new obsession; he just sat alone in his office...and read books and articles and financial filings. He wanted to know, especially, how subprime-mortgage bonds worked" (Lewis 2011, p.26).

Burry's research was exhaustive. "Every mortgage bond came with its own mind-numbingly tedious 130-page prospectus. If you read the fine print, you saw that each bond was its own little corporation. Burry spent the end of 2004 and early 2005 scanning hundreds and actually reading dozens of the prospectuses, certain he was the only one apart from the lawyers who drafted them to do so..." (Lewis 2011, p.27)

At the age of 35, when Burry received his diagnosis of Asperger's Syndrome, "it explained an awful lot about what he did for a living, and how he did it: his obsessive acquisition of hard facts, his insistence on logic, his ability to plow quickly through reams of tedious financial statements. People with Asperger's couldn't control what that they were interested in. It was a stroke of luck that his special interest was financial markets and not, say, collecting lawn mower catalogues" (Lewis 2011, p.183). Burry is quoted as saying, "Only someone who has Asperger's would read a subprime-mortgage-bond prospectus" (p.183).

Michael Burry predicted the subprime mortgage crisis two years before anyone else saw it coming. He found a way to short the market and profit from the subprime implosion. Burry is reported to have made $750 million in 2007 alone, for his investors (2011, p.184).

However, Aspergian special interests do not always translate to viable careers. As I discuss in Chapter 5, it is important to research what tasks the actual jobs involve, and whether an individual can manage them.

Mental rigidity is a well-known characteristic of autism. Aspergians can be quite inflexible in their thinking, insisting on having or doing things in a certain way. Clients have rejected jobs or entire careers because they didn't want to work overtime, *ever*. Some tell me that they persist with disruptive behaviors because they do not want to change. One of my colleagues told me about a man who was looking for a job, but didn't want to wear shoes at work.

A rigid mindset can make it difficult for an individual to cope with novel situations, and to see options. It can get in the way of problem solving.

CLIENT PORTRAIT: SEVEN BUCKETS OF BLEACH ON THE FLOOR

Deborah was a 45-year-old engineer. She was having trouble managing her workload, and coping with the reorganization of her division. She continually described herself as being burned out, exhausted, at the end of her rope and at the point of collapse as a result of working 12-hour days. Deborah lived alone, had no friends and was estranged from her family. As far as I could tell, her psychotherapist was the only other person, aside from myself, whom she interacted with outside of her office.

Deborah gave very precise, detailed descriptions of the situations she wanted to address. She became annoyed if I tried to interrupt. I accepted that this was how she needed to relate events. Her narratives also provided insight into her working style. Every project appeared to have the same importance. I noticed that equal effort went into minor tasks and major assignments. She acknowledged that her co-workers let certain things slide in order to save time. However, she was convinced that if she did, it would backfire. She related two incidents, from years before, when this happened.

We'd had numerous, long discussions about her workload. No matter what I suggested, Deborah came up with a reason why it wouldn't work. She was unwilling to look for another job, saying that she was too tired after work. Weekends were spent resting and catching up with housework and errands.

During one particularly stressful period, Deborah's eyes filled with tears as she described the pressure she was under.

"I'm exhausted when I get home, and by the time I finish cooking, I just go to bed" she said. "There are so many things that I need to take care of, but I just don't have the time."

Having reached an impasse on the job front, I asked Deborah whether it would help to reduce some of the stress in her personal life. She agreed, and wanted to start by figuring out how to have more free time in the evening. Deborah identified meal preparation as a major time drain. We began brainstorming solutions.

Eating in a restaurant was too expensive. Frozen food was out of the question because it didn't taste good. What about take-out? She described three restaurants in her area, and what she might order from each. Problems soon emerged. It would take time to drive to the restaurant. Her food would get cold on the way home. She would have to warm it in the oven. There would be dirty dishes to wash.

Okay, what about the services that deliver high-quality meals, pre-cooked from scratch? We began to volley.

There probably weren't any such companies in her area.

A quick Google search revealed two.

The food would probably be very expensive.

Here's a menu that is reasonably priced.

The meals look fattening.

Not these vegetarian options.

If she worked late, no one would be home to accept the delivery.

Good thing that customers can schedule weekly deliveries.

It will still cost more than cooking something myself.

Yes, but you don't want to spend so much free time cooking.

Now *I* was exhausted and stressed! I got Deborah to agree to contact one of the companies to ask about food delivery, and a trial period.

The following week, Deborah explained that there had been a snag. She had not contacted the meal service that weekend. She had been too busy washing clothes.

"I couldn't believe it," she said, "but it took seven hours on Saturday to wash my blouses so that I would have clean clothes to wear to work this week."

"Wow," I said, "that's a long time to be washing blouses."

"I have to soak them in buckets of water and bleach," Deborah explained. "I had buckets all over my living room!"

She went on to describe a lengthy process of soaking the garments, using a tooth brush to scrub stains, rinsing and hanging the blouses in her bathroom to dry. The next day, she ironed them.

"This is my problem," she said, becoming agitated. "My apartment is a mess, my bills are late, and almost all weekend was spent washing my blouses."

"What about putting them into the washing machine?" I ventured.

"It doesn't get all of the stains out. I get nervous at work, and sweat a lot. The blouses are white," she explained, pointing at the one she was wearing, "so every spot shows."

"What about having them dry cleaned?" I suggested, throwing caution to the wind.

"I tried that once. The dry cleaner couldn't get all of the spots out, either."

"Maybe you could try a different dry cleaner."

I know where this is going, I thought.

"What good would that do?" Deborah countered, "It didn't work last time."

"Suppose you got them dry cleaned, and there were light spots under the arms. How noticeable would those be?" I said.

"I can't wear shirts to work that have spots on them," she insisted.

I've come too far to quit now, I said to myself.

"Maybe you could buy blouses that are colored, or have print fabrics," I said, "that would hide stains."

"I don't have the time or the energy to go shopping," Deborah said.

Score one for Deborah and zero for me.

"It's like we've talked about in the past, Deborah" I said, "if you're not willing to do anything differently, nothing in your life will change."

"I know that I am resistant," she said.

Deborah and I had engaged in a number of similar exchanges during the 16 months that she had been a client. In nearly every coaching session, she declared that she couldn't handle the stress at work much longer. Still, she didn't look for another job, try the meal service or buy clothing that would be easier to keep clean.

A conversation with Deborah's psychotherapist confirmed my suspicions. While depression did cause some of her resistant behavior, she was also extraordinarily rigid in her thinking.

Impact of Inflexibility and Narrow Interests on Employment
An individual may:

- focus on too few, or the wrong details, about an occupation and pursue work that he is unqualified or unsuited for, or that offers limited employment opportunities

- fixate on a particular job or company, and refuse to consider other options

- reject an occupation for the wrong reason, such as not wanting to perform a single undesirable task

- spend too much time pursuing a special interest, neglecting important activities, such as looking for a job

- be unwilling to learn new systems or use new tools; have trouble adapting to change of any kind; insist on doing things his own way

- openly engage in repetitive or self-stimulating behavior, such as hand flapping or rocking, that generates negative attention from co-workers.

SENSORY PROCESSING

Problems with the processing of sensory information are common in autistic individuals (Fein 2011, p.215). Adults in my practice most often complain about over-sensitivity to sights, sounds, odors and tactile sensations.

One of Anne's co-workers smoked. Every time he returned from a cigarette break, the smell of tobacco smoke on his clothing made Anne gag. Since she worked in a very small office at a company with just four employees, she could not move her workspace. She chose to leave the job.

John could not stand the texture of lettuce, or the sound it made when chewed. He was concerned about an upcoming holiday lunch with his co-workers. "If I am offered salad," he asked, "do I have to eat it?"

Several years ago, my office was in a professional building. During a coaching session my client Kim suddenly exclaimed, "Can't you tell the cleaning people to turn off that vacuum cleaner? I can't concentrate!"

Upon hearing her words, I became aware of the soft whir of a vacuum in a distant hallway. Until then, I had been completely unaware of it. But because of Kim's hyper-sensitivity to auditory stimulus, she found the sound of the vacuum to be thoroughly distracting.

Fluorescent lighting is bothersome to many Aspergians, who say that they can see and/or hear the cycling of the bulbs. One man had a strong reaction to the color of fluorescent light. Each day at work, he struggled to ignore the irritating sensation. He was fearful of disclosing his Asperger's Syndrome and requesting an accommodation. One day, to the amusement of his co-workers, he wore a towel on his head to test whether blocking the light made a difference. It did, and he began researching optical lenses that filter fluorescent light.

A light touch, such as a supervisor's supportive tap on the shoulder, can feel unpleasant or painful. The individual may reflexively pull away, or stiffen his body. A woman who could not stand to be hugged by adults welcomed hugs from children. She worked in a daycare center and explained, "Adults don't give you any warning, but I can always tell when the kids are coming and what they want."

When the proprioceptive system is not functioning correctly, an individual will not be aware of where a body part is or how it is moving (Myles *et al.* 2000, p.5). His movements will be poorly coordinated. He might not be able to sit in a chair without looking at it, or know how tightly to grip a pen, or how hard to push a door to close it (p.31). Benjamin couldn't tell how his head was oriented in space. He made eye contact during interviews, but worried that his face might be turned away from the interviewer.

Auditory processing problems can interfere with a person's ability to recognize and interpret what he hears (Attwood 2007, p.221). He may not be able to distinguish background noise from someone's speech. The sound from two or more people talking at once might be perceived as a jumble of words. He might not be able to make sense of rapid speech. Individuals on the autism spectrum often prefer written rather than verbal communications.

The impact of sensory processing abnormalities is not always immediately obvious.

Adam and I were working on job interviewing. I began explaining the importance of eye contact. "This communicates that you are listening…"

"I know that!" Adam interrupted. "But I can't do it."

"Make eye contact?" I asked.

"No, listen."

I thought for a moment.

"Do you mean that you can't look at someone and also listen to what they are saying?"

"Yes," Adam said. "That's why I look at the desk or the wall when someone talks."

Adam seemed relieved when I told him about other clients who had trouble with dual track processing. I related the story of a woman who could not listen and simultaneously write. I showed Adam how to approximate eye contact by looking at the space in between a person's eyebrows.

"Thank you," he said, "for believing me."

In the workplace, sensory sensitivities may be dismissed as pickiness on the part of the Aspergian. Neurotypicals are usually completely unaware that such problems exist, or that a person can experience sensory overload and shut down.

Cyndi described the annual company holiday party as "torture." The crowd of people, loud music, flashing lights and comingled odors of perfume and food made her physically ill. Her supervisor, who knew she had Asperger's Syndrome, refused to let her skip the event, saying that she was being overly dramatic. She summoned all of her strength to attend for a few minutes. The next day her boss criticized her for looking like she didn't want to be there!

Some Aspergians process sensory information more slowly than most people. Several years ago, a colleague and I were exhibiting at an event. Our tables happened to be next to each other. A man walked up to my colleague's table, and the two exchanged a warm greeting. Then the man noticed the bandage around her wrist.

"What happened to your arm?" he asked.

"I fell on some ice and sprained my wrist," she replied.

"Oh," he said, and walked away.

My colleague and I shot each other an amused look.

"*That's* slow processing," she said.

Three or four minutes later, the man returned to my colleague's exhibit table.

"That's awful about your wrist," he said. "Does it hurt?"

How Sensory Challenges Impact Employment

Problems with the processing of sensory information can result in:

- needing to avoid certain physical environments, or to receive accommodations such as a quiet workspace or natural lighting

- productivity problems from not being able to look *and* listen, look *and* write, etc.; job seekers might need to explain such problems at an interview

- overwhelm from too much sensory stimulus, including too many verbal instructions; individual shuts down

- inability to follow group conversations or participate in group discussions without the use of assistive technology; might have to avoid certain occupations

- clumsiness or accidents due to impaired fine and gross muscle control; handwriting might be illegible, or person might write too slowly to take notes in meetings; assembly and other precision hand work may have to be avoided

- anxiety from anticipating or experiencing unpleasant sensations.

EXECUTIVE FUNCTION

Deficits in executive functioning are not part of the diagnostic criteria for an autism spectrum disorder. Nor are they unique to autism. However, they explain several key characteristics of these individuals. These are: repetitive behavior, impulsiveness, lack of mental flexibility and difficulty inhibiting impulses (Frith 2008, p.94).

Although problems with interpersonal communication receive a lot of attention, impaired executive function can be every bit as deleterious. Some of my clients have no difficulties with interpersonal interaction at work, but cannot manage the executive function demands.

Executive function (EF) is generally defined as the cognitive processes required for planning, mental flexibility, inhibition, working memory and fluency (Fein 2011, p.186). These functions are controlled by the frontal lobes of the brain (Frith 2008, p.95). Broadly speaking, the executive functions enable a person to efficiently manage time and resources to get things done.

A popular analogy used to explain EF is that of a busy executive. The executive's job is to initiate, direct and monitor various business initiatives. He establishes goals based on the priorities of stakeholders. He puts plans into place to reach those goals. The plans are based on the careful analysis of information that is relevant to the business, such as sales data, economic forecasts and the activity of competitors.

The executive does not work in a vacuum, but relies on the contributions of employees. He clearly communicates goals and keeps employees motivated and focused on the big picture. He makes sure that their efforts are coordinated. A good leader monitors results and adjusts strategies and plans as needed. If Plan A isn't working, he doesn't panic, react impulsively or keep doing the same thing. He thinks about what he has learned from similar situations in the past. He is flexible, and weighs various options before settling on Plan B.

Even if our executive feels discouraged or uncertain, his outer demeanor projects confidence. He knows that his behavior impacts others and that emotions are contagious. If he is not focused and committed, his employees won't be, either.

As discussed earlier in this chapter, Aspergians have trouble seeing the gist of a situation. In his memoir, *The Journal of Best Practices*, David Finch eloquently describes the Aspergian tendency to hyper-focus on details at the expense of the big picture.

> Everything I want to accomplish is done with the precision of a military operation… To me, a task is a puzzle comprised of a million tiny pieces that must be arranged properly. Usually I find myself more appreciative of the procedure than of the outcome itself. [My wife], on the other hand, sees the process only as the means to an end. I see the trees, in other words, and [my wife] sees the forest. (Finch 2012, p.98)

Finch also relates, with comedic aplomb, the characteristic Aspergian rigidity and resistance to change. Preparing for a business trip, he first has to make arrangements to rent a car. Not any car; a Toyota Camry. Even though he already knows that rental companies will not guarantee a particular model, Finch persists. When a frustrated reservation clerk asks why that model is so critical, he explains:

> "I just prefer to drive a Toyota Camry. I know how they steer, I know where the mirror adjustment thing is, I just…I need a Toyota Camry." My heart was beating heavily, and I repeated myself. "I need a Toyota Camry." … This was how it went with every car rental counter…and how it would go down every time I needed to travel for work. (2012, pp.150–151)

Making a hotel reservation was equally grueling.

> I knew I had to call the hotel before four o'clock because that was when I was most likely to speak with Jennifer, the only person at the front desk who willingly broke her back accommodating my requests. ("Okay, Mr. Finch, we have you all set for one night…I've indicated that you will be arriving in a Toyota Camry, which, again, makes no difference to us… Got you a standard room, king-size bed, nonsmoking, foam pillow, two wake-up calls, and we'll put you as far away from other guests as possible.") (2012, p.153)

The tendency to perseverate (repeat an action or thought well past the precipitating event) is linked to decreased mental flexibility (Fein 2011, p.187). Mark perseverated for months about what he considered to be an inaccurate performance review. Although he had failed to meet several performance benchmarks, he believed that his supervisor was not considering extenuating circumstances. One of these was Mark's insistence on producing work that met his "standard of excellence." He had a difficult time grasping that his job demanded speed rather than exacting precision.

After several attempts with his boss failed to produce a revised review, Mark filed a formal complaint. The matter was now in the hands of the division's vice president, to whom his supervisor reported. After a series of meetings and an analysis of the performance evaluation, the vice president made a decision. The review would stand as originally written.

Still unable to drop the matter, Mark appealed this verdict. He was told, in strong terms, that the discussion was closed.

Four months after the initial review, Mark began working with me, ostensibly to learn strategies for improving his performance. It was soon clear that his real agenda was a revised review. Over several weeks, we examined, in laborious detail, the incidents that led to the negative appraisal. Mark admitted that he had not followed the directives of his boss. We dissected the aspects his performance that she indicated needed to change. Mark agreed that they were realistic and achievable. Still, he wanted a better review.

"According to this email from the vice president, neither she nor your boss will discuss the review," I said. "What about coming up with a plan to address the performance issues, so that you can earn a positive review next time?"

"I don't deserve a rating of 'didn't meet expectations,'" Mark fumed, "I *exceeded* the quality standards in order to keep our customers happy."

"My concern, Mark, is that you are perseverating on the review. You've been told that the matter is closed. If you keep bringing it up, you could jeopardize your job," I said.

When the session ended, Mark was clearly upset. The next day, he emailed me to say that he would not continue with the coaching. A year later, I happened upon a notice from a business networking Web site saying that Mark was working at a different company.

Perseveration consumes mental energy and distracts people from their real priorities. Job seekers may become obsessed with jobs that are unrealistic, or with working for a specific company. One man was fixated on working at IBM in the management training program. He repeatedly mentioned this goal, even though he did not meet any of the requirements.

Autistic individuals often have trouble planning the steps that are needed to reach a goal (Fein 2011, p.194). Specific tasks, such as writing a résumé, must be methodically broken down into specific actions. If the first step isn't clear, the individual will more than likely not even attempt the task. I observed this so consistently with my clients that I am now in the habit of asking, "What is the first thing that you need to do?"

The *concept* of time may be poorly understood (Meltzer 2010, p.71). Many of my clients are not able to accurately estimate how long tasks will take, or whether they are possible to achieve within a certain time period.

Steven was preparing to begin his junior year of college. He wanted to improve his ability to schedule projects, particularly term papers. He set up visual and auditory reminders on his smart phone. Yet he consistently wound up working throughout the night to meet deadlines.

"Tell me exactly what you do when you schedule a paper," I said.

It turned out that Steven merely entered the *project* due date on his calendar. He did not organize the various steps, such as researching and editing, and allot time for them. No wonder he was pulling all nighters! We spent the rest of his coaching session identifying all of the tasks related to writing a term paper, and estimating how long he would need for each. I showed him how to work backward from the final due date to create a project timeline.

Inhibition is an executive function that enables a person to stop certain thoughts or actions at the appropriate time. It allows attention to be focused on what is relevant, while the irrelevant is disregarded (Fein 2011, p.189). An employee may need to stop working on an interesting project in order to attend to a pressing matter. Or, he might need to concentrate on an assignment instead of the date he has that evening.

An executive function deficit common among Aspergians is poor impulse control. Individuals often blurt out the first thought that comes to mind, without thinking about whether it is appropriate. Or, they react impetuously, without considering the consequences of their actions (Barkley 2011, p.43). Poor emotional regulation (Frith 2008, p.94) can also jeopardize employment.

Samantha typifies the impact of poor inhibition, impulse control and emotional regulation. She would plan to take a five-minute break at work, then realize that she had spent 20 minutes surfing the Internet. Because she became lost following interesting tangents that were not related to her work, she frequently missed deadlines.

Co-workers considered Samantha to be immature. She would impulsively ask questions to which she could easily find the answers. She treated every new assignment as an emergency. Samantha would drop what she had been working on then begin muttering, "I'll never get this done!" When she was frustrated, she would curse or begin to cry.

Samantha noticed that, during breaks, her colleagues would stop talking if she came near. When she asked, "Why are you ignoring me?" they denied the accusation and returned to their desks. Samantha didn't understand why she was never invited to lunch.

During a staff meeting, the subject of teamwork came up. Samantha blurted out, "Are you kidding? There's no teamwork at this company!"

Working memory is considered to be the most important executive function (Meltzer 2010, p.112). It is believed to act as the "central executive" that directs other cognitive processes, such as attention shifting, inhibition and direction of mental effort (2010, p.113).

Working memory allows a person to hold and manipulate information for short periods of time, while completing a task (Gathercole and Alloway 2008, p.2). The amount of data that can be held in the working memory is limited. The average adult can retain up to seven pieces of information (2008, pp.3–4). Mental arithmetic and recalling a friend's telephone number are examples of tasks that require the use of working memory.

Working memory is essential for performing many tasks in the workplace:

- remembering the steps in a procedure, specific aspects of a task, verbal instructions

- recalling pertinent details in order to comprehend the meaning of written material

- writing, including the correct spelling of words, recalling words to use in a sentence and organizing a paragraph

- mental arithmetic, such as remembering sums in multi-step computations

- recalling important information during note taking

- remembering instructions.

(Meltzer 2010, p.114)

Individuals on the autism spectrum have weaker working memory than neurotypicals (Gaus 2011, p.49). This explains their difficulty with multitasking. When interrupted during a task, they have trouble re-orienting themselves, and perhaps even remembering the original task. As one client explained, "I lose my place, and have to start all over again."

Strong executive functioning is characterized by mental flexibility and the capacity to see options. These abilities are especially important for solving problems. *Fluency* describes a person's ability to produce multiple examples within a certain category. Verbal fluency, for example, can be tested by asking someone to come up with as many words as possible that start with the letter "b," within a certain time period (Fein 2011, p.194). Generating multiple responses to a problem is a complex type of fluency.

Individuals on the autism spectrum struggle to see options and generate novel solutions to problems (Frith 2008, p.98). Some individuals cannot cope when a customary course of action fails to produce a result (p.99). When a cash register wasn't working, an Aspergian clerk kept trying to complete the transaction. He was oblivious to the growing line of impatient shoppers. It didn't occur to him to seek help from a manager.

Andrew's supervisor was frustrated by the errors he made when attempting to reconcile receipts. She said that if his accuracy did not improve he would lose his job.

"The problem is that I forget a step, or do them in the wrong order, and then the numbers are off," Andrew said. He went on to give an example.

"It sounds like you are relying on your memory, which isn't reliable," I said. "What could you do to remind yourself of all the steps, and their proper sequence?"

Andrew was stumped. "I do the best that I can to remember," he said.

"What about creating a check list?" I prompted.

Andrew agreed that this was a good idea. We created a list with boxes he could check after completing each step. Within three weeks of implementing this change, his supervisor complimented Andrew on his accuracy.

In the 13 years that he had worked in the high technology field, Martin had lost six jobs. He could not work quickly enough to meet deadlines. Yet he continued pursuing the same type of job. I asked whether he wanted to explore transferring his skills to a less pressured occupation. Martin was stunned. "I never thought of that before!" he exclaimed, proceeding to thank me profusely for my insight.

How Executive Function Challenges Impact Employment

Deficits in executive functioning hamper the productivity of both job seekers and employees. Common challenges include:

- *difficulty learning a new job:* individual cannot learn processes or procedures quickly enough; cannot remember individuals steps; is unable to meet productivity requirements (works too slowly); doesn't grasp aspects of the job others consider to be obvious

- *poor concept of time:* unable to accurately estimate how long a task should take; unclear about what can be accomplished in a particular amount of time; loses track of time; often misses deadlines or is late to appointments

- *appears to lack initiative:* unable to infer what is needed; finishes a task and waits for further instructions; doesn't begin assignment if first steps are not clear; asks too many questions in attempt to clarify expectations; doesn't try to seek answers on his own

- *problems prioritizing and multitasking:* spends time on unimportant tasks; does not seek short cuts or alternatives; does not adjust content based on audience or end-user needs; forgets place in a project if interrupted; forgets commitments; becomes confused or overwhelmed trying to manage multiple activities at once

- *difficulty planning and organizing:* unable to plan an effective job search or projects at work; can't execute details and keep an eye on the big picture; unsure of what the finished product should look like; inefficient systems for keeping track of information

- *ineffective problem solving:* repeats what isn't working; doesn't learn from past mistakes; re-invents the wheel; reacts impulsively or based on too little information; doesn't ask for help; when unsure of what action to take, does nothing

- *poor emotional control:* reactions are out of proportion to events; acts without considering options or consequences; little motivation to complete tasks that are not interesting.

Chapter 2

ANXIETY, ANGER AND OTHER EMOTIONS

The difficulty that Aspergians have understanding, expressing and regulating emotions (Attwood 2007, p.129) has far-reaching impact in the workplace. Inappropriate displays of anger, frustration or unhappiness make co-workers uncomfortable, and can be grounds for dismissal. When the innocent actions of colleagues are misinterpreted as hostile the Aspergian risks alienating his work mates. Anxiety drives impulsive actions that may lead, ultimately, to job loss.

To the degree that an individual has trouble understanding and managing emotions, he may:

- not recognize whether or when others are upset or angry with him

- know that others are upset, but not understand why or how to respond

- believe that he is the reason others are distressed, when this is clearly not the case

- misinterpret or mislabel another person's emotional state

- over-react to minor events, behaving in ways that are immature, intimidating or threatening to others.

When neurotypicals describe personal experiences, they are usually framed in terms of how the person felt. In contrast, Aspergians tend to relate facts rather than feelings. It can appear that the individual does not have emotions. Upsetting events may be told in a matter-of-fact way, accompanied by a neutral facial expression. This should not be interpreted to mean that he does not have strong feelings. He may struggle to identify and express his emotions, a condition known as *alexithymia* (Attwood 2007, p.130). Or, they may be expressed in unusual ways. When Kate described troubling events, she would bend forward in her chair, her face almost touching her knees, then snap upright. When Kyle felt happy, he would start skipping—atypical behavior for a 34-year-old in an office.

Kathy was disappointed to learn that she had not been selected for an entry-level position with a well-known research library. Several months before, at age 31, she had earned a master's degree in library science and was eager to start her career.

Her diagnosis of Asperger's Syndrome came in high school. It helped explain her awkwardness around her classmates, and uneven academic performance. In particular, she struggled with classes related to social studies and English. Reading fiction was "a nightmare" because she couldn't follow the story lines (too much left to the imagination) or grasp the emotional reactions of the characters. The stories simply didn't make sense.

However, Kathy loved to categorize and organize information. "My brain is black-and-white," she explained, "so I like rules."

With extra tutoring and great effort on her part, Kathy finished high school and then went on to earn a bachelor's degree in five years. She volunteered in the college library and enjoyed it so much that she decided to pursue a master's degree in library science.

Kathy was particularly sensitive about finding a job because her younger brother had already established himself in a career. She said that he had recently been promoted. Then, the tears came. "I feel like the failure in the family," she sobbed.

I shifted the discussion to Kathy's accomplishments, reminding her that anyone who earns a master's degree is not a failure. I gave her an assignment for the next week: list ten things she did well.

"No one knows what I went through to get that master's degree," she said.

"From what you have described, it took a lot," I said. "What if we make that another assignment; to write down what it took to get the degree," I suggested.

"Okay!" she said, her face brightening.

The following week Kathy returned for her coaching session. We reviewed her list of accomplishments, which included the distinction of Most Helpful in third grade. Then, it was time to review her journey to a graduate degree. Kathy opened her notebook and began reading.

For a moment, I was taken aback. Then I caught myself and thought, *Of course! She has Asperger's Syndrome.*

I had readied myself for a wrenching narrative about Kathy's personal struggles and hardships. Instead, she matter-of-factly recited what, indeed, it had taken to earn the master's degree: speaking with a professor about accommodations for tests; writing outlines for papers, receiving feedback and rewriting the outlines; memorizing cataloging systems; giving presentations in class. The two pages of neatly lettered bullet points contained not a single emotional recollection!

These individuals often have limited ability to identify and describe subtle emotional states (Attwood 2007, p.144). Their interactions with others may be misinterpreted or misreported.

When I first started working with people who have Asperger's, I was surprised by how often clients would say that their supervisors "yell and scream at me." These dramatic reactions didn't match the situations they described. I probed to get a better idea what happened when a boss yelled and screamed. What does he say? Is his voice loud? Is his face red? Invariably, it turned out that the individual received some type of feedback, but the boss did not actually raise his voice.

I was with a young man named Rick at a library, preparing to reserve a study room. There was no one at the front desk. We noticed a woman in a nearby office, talking on the telephone. We could see her through the large pane of glass in her office door. We waited at the desk for about five minutes before she finished her call and came out to assist us.

Key to the study room in hand, we made our way across the library to meet Rick's mother. She was going to join us for part of the coaching session. She asked what took us so long to get the key. "The lady was screaming at someone on the phone," Rick said.

Even though we could not hear what the librarian was saying, it was clear from her body language that she was not having a heated discussion. We used the incident as a lesson in nonverbal communication, although I was not able to ascertain why Rick thought the librarian was screaming.

Parents, and professionals who work with this population, are familiar with the term "meltdown." It refers to the severe emotional reactions common to individuals on the autism spectrum. While meltdowns are typically associated with children, adults can also lose emotional control. This can happen suddenly: the individual is fine one moment and then explodes in anger and frustration the next.

Research suggests that structural and functional abnormalities in the amygdala may explain the difficulty that people with Asperger's Syndrome have regulating emotions. According to Tony Attwood in *The Complete Guide to Asperger's Syndrome*:

> This can explain why the child or adult does not appear to be consciously aware of increasing emotional stress, and his or her thoughts and behavior are not indicative of deterioration in mood. Eventually the degree of emotion or stress is overwhelming, but it may be too late for the cognitive or thoughtful control of the emotion. There were no early warning signals of an emotional meltdown in observable behavior that could be used by another person to repair the mood, or warning signals in the conscious thoughts of the person with Asperger's syndrome [sic] to enable him or her to use self-control. (2007, p.145).

The irritability, explosive outbursts and frequent mood swings associated with poor emotional regulation (Gaus 2007, p.32) can interfere with productivity in the workplace. The individual may not know how to handle conflicts with co-workers, or deal with disappointing news. Clients have lost jobs because they over-reacted to being denied the use of vacation time on a holiday weekend. Generally, I notice that clients who have serious problems with emotional control are in jobs that require frequent and sophisticated interaction with others.

Certainly, individuals can learn to control their emotional reactions, and I discuss tools that I find effective in Chapter 7. Sometimes, the solution is for the individual to find an occupation that is less stressful. Cognitive behavioral therapy (CBT) has been shown to be effective for treating mood disorders in individuals with Asperger's Syndrome (Attwood 2007, p.151). Obviously, treatment of mood disorders requires the services of a clinician.

Aspergians are said to lack empathy and find this characterization to be hurtful and insulting. They argue that they are kind, sensitive and care about other people. And they are completely correct. I do not believe that Aspergians lack empathy; I see them as empathic in an intellectual way.

Several years ago, I discussed "the empathy question" with a lovely man who has Asperger's Syndrome. He explained, "I usually need a few minutes to think through why someone is upset. Then I can empathize."

Autism researcher Simon Baron-Cohen describes this as a difference between affective and cognitive empathy. According to Baron-Cohen, the affective empathy of people on the autism spectrum is intact. When they understand a person's state of mind, they are able to respond in an emotionally proper way. The problem is with cognitive empathy, which requires the ability to identify another person's state of mind. Without cognitive empathy a person cannot *instinctively* respond to another's distress (Baron-Cohen 2011, p.3).

The greater degree to which an individual has problems understanding the thoughts, feelings and perspectives of others (see theory of mind in Chapter 1), the more he will struggle to respond to situations in the right way. He may give the impression of being cold or uncaring when the opposite is true.

Natalie worked as an aide at a facility serving children with profound physical disabilities. In December, a small group of children went to the theatre to enjoy a holiday show. During intermission, Natalie took one of the children to the rest room. The seven-year-old girl was unable to walk, feed herself or speak.

As Natalie was washing her hands the attendant asked, "Do you need help with the baby?"

Infuriated, Natalie replied, "She is *not* a baby!" and proceeded to lecture the attendant on why she should not treat persons with disabilities so disrespectfully.

Even though I was not there, I could imagine that a young child with such severe physical problems was probably quite small. In a wheelchair, viewed from across a room at a certain angle, the child may have appeared to be age two or younger. It was clear that the attendant intended no disrespect.

Natalie's ire was evident even in her retelling. I'm sure the attendant was confused and hurt by Natalie's reaction to her offer of help. Even sketching the scene to give Natalie a visual of different perspectives didn't help her to see the situation differently.

Poor perspective taking cost Bob a part-time job on his very first day. His supervisor brought Bob to his cubicle, and turned on the computer he would be using. While the computer was booting up, she showed Bob how to use the telephone.

Turning her attention back to the computer she said, "It usually loads faster than this."

"It's not my fault!" Bob exclaimed.

"No one said it was your fault," she answered.

"You just did!" Bob insisted.

The manager told Bob that she didn't like his attitude and he was escorted from the premises.

As we debriefed the incident Bob explained, "Because so many people have thought that I am incompetent, I assumed that she was blaming me because the computer didn't work."

It can be quite disturbing to an Aspergian when others do not agree with his opinions, ideals or method for accomplishing a task. Evan became thoroughly disenchanted with being a federal employee. Craving order, structure and "clear rules of conduct," he presumed that anyone working for the government would share his patriotic zeal. He was stunned that his co-workers were not interested in discussions about democracy.

"How can you work for your government, and not care about something like that?" he asked incredulously. After repeated, passionate attempts to engage others in his interest, several complained to the human resources department. To Evan, this was unconscionable. Unable to tolerate such closed-mindedness, he quit shortly afterward.

Attwood also states that an individual "may have an unusual or immature concept of emotions in terms of understanding that someone can have two feelings at the same time..." (2007, p.134). This can make it more difficult to understand the intentions of others. A person may not realize that a supervisor can be annoyed by a behavior, but still think that he is doing a good job.

Joseph and I were working on body language; in particular, his ability to notice and correctly interpret the more obvious signals. To practice, we watched short clips on YouTube with the sound turned off. Joseph would guess what was happening, and what the characters were feeling based on their body language and contextual clues. Clips from soap operas provided plenty of obvious emotional drama to work with.

One scenario involved a young couple who had a fight. Joseph correctly guessed that the young man and woman were angry with each other. He knew that the woman had discovered something upsetting about her mate. Now, in the presence of the husband's or wife's parents, the young man was asking for forgiveness.

I congratulated Joseph for his nonverbal acumen, reviewing all of the signals that he had correctly interpreted.

"You can really learn a lot about how people feel by noticing their body language," Joseph commented.

"Yes, it's amazing," I agreed, adding, "and isn't it interesting how different people can react differently to the same situation?"

I was referring to the older couple in the clip, who emerged as parents of the young woman. The mother was actively encouraging the couple to reconcile. The father merely looked up from his newspaper two or three times, suggesting that fighting was a familiar scenario.

This was novel information to 33-year-old Joseph. "I never thought of that," he said.

Erin's story illustrates how emotional reactions to misunderstandings can jeopardize the efforts of job seekers.

After finishing her junior year at a prestigious university, Erin landed a coveted summer internship at an investment bank. She and her fellow interns had been invited to attend the annual employee picnic. Initially, Erin did not plan to attend. She was uncomfortable in groups and with starting conversations. "As you know, my Asperger's makes it hard for me to understand people," she said.

Her parents, who were both successful professionals, convinced Erin that the outing would be an excellent networking opportunity. "My father says that I should introduce myself to the vice president of my division," she said, "so that later on I can send him my résumé."

To her credit, Erin pushed past her anxiety and attended the picnic. Almost immediately, she saw Meghan, the vice president's executive assistant. Meghan had extended the invitations to the interns. Erin had asked in their email exchange if Meghan would arrange an introduction to the vice president. Meghan had replied that she would try to set something up.

Erin walked up to Meghan and introduced herself.

"Isn't that your boss?" she asked, pointing to a man near the refreshment table.

Meghan turned to scan the crowd and replied, "He's busy right now. I'll try to catch him when he's free." She returned to her conversation with a group of co-workers.

As the picnic continued Erin grew increasingly anxious. Spotting Meghan, she asked again about an introduction to the vice president.

"I don't know where he is," Meghan said, obviously annoyed. "If I see him, I'll let him know that you want to talk to him."

Erin was angry.

"I couldn't believe it," she said. "Meghan *knew* that it was important for me to meet the vice president. She never did set up an introduction. I think Meghan owes me an apology!"

As we dissected the picnic, Erin took notes. I could see that she was struggling to understand what had transpired.

"The reason that you went to the picnic was to meet the vice president," I said. "But for Meghan it was a social event and a chance to have fun with her co-workers. I'm sure that she made an effort to help you out. But it wouldn't be right to expect that she would take responsibility for arranging an introduction for you."

"What you could do," I continued, "is email her a thank you for inviting you to the picnic, and ask whether she could arrange a brief meeting with the vice president before your internship ends."

Erin agreed to do this, although I do not think she completely understood the reasoning behind my suggestion. She also wanted to discuss feedback that she had received from the woman who supervised the interns. The supervisor said that Erin needed to improve her teamwork skills.

"When someone gives me a new assignment, I get annoyed," Erin said. "I have to work on one thing at a time. I need time to think about whether I can handle another project."

"When you hesitate or sound irritated, what message are you sending to the person who wants you to do the assignment?" I asked.

Erin thought for a while. "That I don't want to do it, and that I'm not a team player," she replied. "I *want* to do the work. I just need to figure out whether I can."

We came up with a different strategy for Erin. She would immediately say yes to assignments. Later, she would think through whether she could handle them, and speak to her supervisor if there was a problem. We did some role playing so that she could practice sounding enthusiastic instead of annoyed when accepting projects.

The elevated levels of anxiety that are so common among individuals with Asperger's Syndrome obviously cause difficulties for job seekers and employees. It is not known whether anxiety is a feature of Asperger's, or the result of an individual trying to cope in the neurotypical world. In my opinion, it is mostly the latter.

Patty works part-time in a retail store, and sometimes hides from customers to avoid interacting with strangers. Matt's supervisor corrected a minor error in his work, and now Matt is certain that he will be fired. Jill is nervous about talking on the telephone, and does not return calls from potential employers responding to her résumé.

A change in routine can trigger anxiety (Attwood 2007, p.136). Alex admitted ambivalence about working. He wanted to use his skills and earn money, yet he worried about upsetting his usual daily schedule. Individuals who are employed may panic when there is a new schedule, process or supervisor.

The Aspergian might envision problems where there aren't any. Matt is typical. He feared losing his job over a single, minor mistake, even though he had worked at the company for more than three years, and had very good performance reviews.

Social situations are obvious anxiety triggers. Typically, the fear is not knowing what to say, or of saying or doing the wrong thing. One client summed up his anxiety about interacting with co-workers: "Going into work is like walking into a war zone."

Perfectionist tendencies may cause an individual to be distraught at the prospect of making a mistake. He may experience great anxiety about making decisions, fearing that they will be wrong.

Yet another source of anxiety is sensory sensitivities. A person may fret about possibly encountering a noise, odor or other painful or noxious stimulus (Attwood 2007, p.136). Sometimes, simply being surrounded by other people is very uncomfortable.

CLIENT PORTRAIT: PANIC AND PARANOIA

Wesley contacted me in a state of "panic and paranoia" that he was about to lose his job. The precipitating event was an upcoming performance review.

"My boss must realize that I am incompetent," he said, "and that I've been faking it all these years."

Wesley was an electronics engineer. He was initially drawn to the profession because of a fascination with consumer electronics. For nearly a quarter century, he worked on new technologies, designing complex electronics systems. He had been with his current employer for 12 years.

According to Wesley, he had been bored with the work for about a decade. Within the past six months, he had been having a greater difficulty "faking" interest in his work.

"I haven't kept my skills current," he said, "and a lot of the time, I don't know what I am doing. My title is Senior Electronics Engineer, but really I am a junior engineer."

Recently, a colleague had complained that Wesley asked too many questions. "He told me to look up the answer in the documentation," Wesley said, "but I was too panicked to focus on reading. Now, I'm afraid that my co-worker will tell my boss that I am incompetent."

Wesley explained that interactions with co-workers, even via email, made him nervous. Despite his years on the job, he had no friends in the office. "I just want to be left alone." When he wasn't busy, Wesley worried that he would be let go. When he was working on a project, he feared not performing the tasks perfectly.

"You've had the same supervisor for almost a decade," I said, "and he has never complained about your productivity."

"He says that my performance pressure is self-created," Wesley admitted. "My boss says that I am doing fine, but I don't believe him."

At one point, Wesley commented that he didn't feel capable of living independently as an adult. When I observed that he had been living on his own for 25 years, he looked surprised. "I don't *feel* like a grown up," he said.

He went on to describe his panic whenever he did not know how to handle a task. "I need to be told what to do," he said. "I don't know some of the computer applications very well."

"It sounds like bringing your skills up to date would eliminate a lot of stress on the job," I said. "How can you get the training you need?"

"I could take courses, but I have no interest in learning more," Wesley said. "What I really want is a job where there are no expectations." He paused and smiled. "I guess that's not realistic."

A psychotherapist had given Wesley some insight.

"She told me that because of my Asperger's, my thinking is black-and-white," he said. "She also says that I am too negative."

"I hear a lot of all-or-nothing thinking," I agreed. "It also seems like you perseverate on the negatives, and what could go wrong."

Over the course of several weeks, we looked for evidence that Wesley was about to be fired, and found none. His previous performance reviews were largely positive. It did not appear that his co-worker had said anything to Wesley's supervisor about his asking too many questions. Wesley's projects were completed on time and there were no complaints about quality.

Despite all of his apprehension, Wesley's latest performance review was again positive and he was given a raise. His supervisor did comment that he wanted Wesley to interact more with his colleagues. "He says that every year," observed Wesley.

The review out of the way for another year, Wesley decided that he wanted to find a different career that would be less stressful. Once again, Wesley saw one problem after another: his interests (Anime and Greek history) wouldn't translate to well paid work; he didn't have enough money to earn another four-year degree; he would be too tired to pursue a certificate program in the evening; any career wouldn't work if he didn't earn at least his current salary.

I wondered aloud whether a different career was really the solution to Wesley's distress. We eventually agreed that the priority was finding a way to manage his anxiety. I referred him to a psychotherapist who specializes in treating individuals on the autism spectrum.

It is estimated that one in three individuals with Asperger's Syndrome is clinically depressed (Attwood 2007, p.140). This is not surprising to me, given the amount of stress in their lives. Many individuals had difficult childhoods where they were criticized, teased and ostracized by their peers. Some experience the same treatment as adults.

These adults may also have poor social support systems, and suffer from loneliness and isolation. There are times when it is clear to me that I, perhaps along with a psychotherapist, am the primary confidant in a person's life.

David and I were working on his interviewing skills. He was highly motivated, extroverted and talkative. After finishing up the list of assignments for the coming week, I asked David who could help him practice.

"How about a friend, who can do a role play with you?" I asked.

Suddenly, David's face grew tense. He looked down at his notepad. I noticed that his eyelids were fluttering. Thinking that it might be a seizure, I was silent for about 30 seconds.

"Are you okay?" I asked softly.

David nodded yes.

"What's the matter?"

"I don't *have* any friends," David said, "and don't want to start crying."

From that day forward, I changed the way that I make such inquiries. Now I ask, "Who do you know who could help?"

Protracted job searches chip away at self-esteem, which can lead to depression. So does working in a job that doesn't utilize one's intellect. Repeated job loss creates financial stress, as well as feelings of shame and embarrassment. Like Sisyphus, the individual's best efforts fail to produce results.

Neurotypicals, with all good intentions, may attempt to cheer a person up or help him look on the bright side by minimizing what appear to be minor concerns. This of course makes the Aspergian feel worse.

I remember an earnest young man who wanted a job but was concerned about working nine to five. That schedule would mean that he could not eat dinner at the customary hour. The casual observer might conclude that he lacked motivation, and wasn't serious about finding employment. Neither of these was true. A predictable routine was very important to him.

I did not treat this as a trivial concern. Instead, I acknowledged his worry and validated his desire to eat dinner at the usual time. After that, we got into problem solving mode. Happily, after weighing the pros and cons this man decided that the benefits of working outweighed the discomfort of adopting a new meal time.

Approximately half of the individuals in my coaching practice also work with a clinician to address anxiety, depression and other mental health problems. For some, like Wesley, addressing a mental health condition is a prerequisite to coaching. Seeking treatment is important. Several clients have told me that it was only after they started taking anti-anxiety medication that they were able to be around other people and consider getting jobs.

Chapter 3

UTILIZING STRENGTHS WITHIN THE WORKPLACE

This book has described the differences in how people on the autism spectrum process information, and the challenges this creates in the workplace. However, these differences are also strengths when individuals are in the right jobs and receive the right supports.

There are many occupations that utilize the abilities of people with Asperger's Syndrome. I think of neurotypicals and Aspergians as filling different and complementary roles within the workplace. Neurotypicals are the multitasking generalists, and Aspergians are the specialists, technicians and experts.

Neurotypicals possess broad skill sets and are able to manage many different kinds of tasks. Aspergians develop expertise in more narrowly defined areas. The former excel at selling ideas and communicating within a group. The latter can be counted on to take care of the details and work independently.

David has worked at a small kitchen and bath product dealership for a decade. During this time he has acquired encyclopedic knowledge of the company and its products. The owner marvels at his ability to recall part numbers, his accuracy with inventory, and his memory of events that happened several years ago. "I'm afraid to lose him," she says, "because he knows so much."

Frank has never missed a single day of work in the three years he has been at the hardware store. He can direct customers to any item within the store from memory.

Cara is a master trouble shooter thanks to her remarkably in-depth knowledge of her company's purchasing processes. She can recite complex procedures and employees describe her ability to spot inefficiencies as "legendary."

Although every individual is unique, there are certain strengths associated with the autistic style of thinking and perceiving. I have observed these patterns in clients, regardless of their jobs or income level.

Aspergians are well known for strong logic and analytic skills. These are attributable to the bottom-up processing style that is characteristic of (but not exclusive to) autistic individuals (Frith 2003, p.163).

Bottom-up processing is data driven. An individual analyses information from the physical senses based on its own merit. Various pieces of data are pieced together and then a conclusion is drawn (Fritscher 2014). Top-down processing is conceptually driven. Meaning is derived from context, knowledge, memory and past experience (Cherry 2014a). Neurotypicals tend to favor top-down processing.

Suppose that you receive directions to drive one mile to an intersection. At the traffic light you are to make a right turn, by the Exxon gasoline station. You set out, and when your odometer registers one mile, you come to an intersection and stop at a red light. The only gasoline station you see is Mobil. What would you do?

If you are neurotypical, you would probably turn right at the Mobil station. Your decision would be based on:

- the expectation that you will turn right after driving one mile

- seeing the intersection, traffic light and *a* gasoline station

- your knowledge that Exxon and Mobil are both gasoline stations

- past experiences where you have confused the names of convenience stores.

This is big picture, top-down processing.

It is likely that an Aspergian would keep driving, seeking a sign for Exxon. He would be matching all of the specific details: distance, traffic light, right turn, Exxon station. He thinks, "How could someone confuse Exxon with Mobil?" This is data driven, bottom-up processing.

Dr. Laurent Mottron is a clinician and researcher in Canada whose focus is the cognitive neuroscience of autism. In an article in *Nature* magazine, "The Power of Autism," he describes an "autism advantage" in certain jobs, such as scientific research.

Dr. Mottron has worked with several autistic individuals, one of whom has been his co-author on over a dozen papers. He says that many autistics are well suited for science because of their interest in processes, ability to see patterns, and intense focus. His co-author was largely self-taught and "deserves a PhD" (Mottron 2011, p.33).

One of the benefits of his collaborator's bottom-up style is that "ideas come from the available facts, and from them only," which results in work that is very accurate. Dr. Mottron contrasts this to his top-down processing style, where he begins with a hypothesis and then looks for facts that support or refute it. "Combining the two types of brains in the same research group is amazingly productive" (2011, p.35).

Individuals on the autism spectrum are described as detail-oriented because of this bottom-up processing style. It enables them to perceive complex patterns, and to analyze data impartially, which can reveal insights or solutions that other people miss. It is also why many excel at spotting errors and anomalies in large sets of data.

Other autistic strengths are the ability to hyper-focus on a task for extended periods of time, and a high tolerance for repetition and routine. These traits are assets in many occupations, such as: scientific and academic research, computer programming, writing, assembly work, statistical analysis, fine arts and crafts such as weaving and painting, and data entry. This does not mean that an individual will *never* tire of a task; but the threshold of boredom is higher.

In the workplace, excellent long-term memory for facts and events enables these employees to amass vast stores of institutional knowledge. One of my clients is regularly consulted to explain why certain processes were put into place, including some from almost 20 years ago!

Aspergians will stick with a job until it is done. Their work style is usually methodical, resulting in high quality, accurate work. They are faithful followers of rules and procedures. *They want to do a good job and do it right.*

The Aspergian traits of honesty and loyalty are universally valued by employers. They can be counted on to tell the truth as they see it, even when it is not politically correct or does not advance their own interests. After working in corporate environments for two decades, I'll argue that many organizations would benefit from employees who aren't afraid to say when the emperor has no clothes!

Their inherent dislike of change means that when they find the right job, Aspergians stay put. An employer who invests in training for them will likely have loyal employees for years to come.

Finally, Aspergians are smart. One feature that differentiated Asperger's Syndrome from autism (prior to 2013) was the absence of cognitive impairment.

Many Aspergians have intellectual capability that is above average, and sometimes in the superior range. Interestingly, autistic individuals outperform neurotypicals in the Raven's Matrices intelligence test. This test requires the use of analytic skills to complete visual patterns. In one experiment, autistics were 40 percent faster in completing the test (Mottron 2011, p.34).

For almost 15 years, Allan has been a project manager at a major, international corporation. His primary responsibility is to develop efficient processes for product development. The industry is governed by many rules and regulations. Introducing new products is a long and complex undertaking.

Since Allan knows the industry and the company's products so well, he can predict, with great accuracy, problems that will arise when a procedure isn't followed. Allan takes his job very seriously. When he creates a process, he carefully examines each step, from many different angles. He sees his job as creating the best, most efficient system possible.

To Allan, following procedures is a rule that should never be broken. He finds it difficult to hide his irritation at those who do not comply. Realizing that Allan is no diplomat, his boss now steps in when one of "Allan's rules" must be enforced. This is an excellent example of Aspergians and neurotypicals balancing each other out. Allan's supervisor recognizes all of his abilities, and takes over the social interaction that he finds to be difficult.

SOCIAL ENTERPRISES ARE GOOD BUSINESS

Today, innovative organizations are creating employment opportunities that take advantage of the specialized skills of people on the autism spectrum.

Specialisterne pioneered this concept in 2004. Founded in Denmark by Thorkil Sonne, whose son has Asperger's Syndrome, the company trains individuals on the autism spectrum as software testers. Sonne conceived the idea after realizing that, in addition to challenges, his son possesses specific abilities. Software testing utilizes autistic strengths: focus, attention to detail and precision. Specialisterne (which is Danish for "the specialists") outsources testing services to clients such as Microsoft and Oracle.

Specialisterne has expanded operations in Europe, and in 2012, established a presence in the United States. Sonne formed The Specialist People Foundation with the goal of creating one million jobs around the world for "specialist people" with autism and similar challenges (see www.specialisterne.com).

Aspiritech (www.aspiritech.org) was founded in 2008 by Brenda and Moshe Weitzberg, who are also parents of a son with Asperger's Syndrome. Aspiritech trains and employs individuals on the autism spectrum as software testers. It provides outsourced testing services to client companies.

Aspiritech receives hundreds of applications annually from individuals across the world. Those who are accepted possess a basic fluency in computers, and live within a reasonable commuting distance from the organization's suburban Chicago office. The on-site training lasts for about one month. Testers learn how to use test scripts to find bugs in software, and then advance to creating their own scripts.

Individuals who successfully complete the training are hired by Aspiritech. Almost all work part-time. Some go on to full-time jobs at other companies. Aspiritech matches projects from client companies to the abilities of each tester. For example, some testers visit client sites to discuss projects. However, for some Aspiritech employees, face-to-face meetings or even telephone calls would be quite stressful. For this reason, Aspiritech utilizes cloud-based spreadsheets which enable client communication to happen over the Internet.

Aspiritech provides its testers with written material to augment verbal instructions. They also refer to "cheat sheets" with step-by-step outlines of a process. The employees have access to a quiet room with sensory equipment to avoid becoming overwhelmed.

Aspiritech has worked with nearly 30 client companies, and nearly all are repeat customers. It markets both its mission to employ autistic workers and the quality of the services those workers provide. According to Marc Lazar, Aspiritech's Autism Specialist, clients comment that the testers "find bugs that others don't even think to look for." He adds that managers and executives at Aspiritech's client companies often have personal connections to someone on the autism spectrum.

Similar organizations exist in other parts of the United States, and in other countries. They include ULTRA Testing in New York City, AQA in Israel, Kaien in Japan and seeDetail in the United Kingdom. More are sure to follow.

The Specialists Guild (http://specialistsguild.org) provides job training and internships that prepare autistic individuals for meaningful careers. Founded in San Francisco in 2011, The Specialists Guild (TSG) currently offers training in software testing. After completing ten weeks of instruction, individuals develop their skills through contract and pro-bono projects. They work for approximately one year as paid TSG interns. Interns receive instruction on communication and other "soft skills."

When internships are completed, TSG works with individuals to secure permanent jobs.

Founders Andy and Luby Aczel chose to focus on software testing because of Andy's background in the high technology industry. They encourage others to adapt their model within their local communities. There are three steps:

1. Identify jobs that are in demand within the community.

2. Provide access to training.

3. Partner with businesses to provide projects for internships.

Occupations must obviously be a match for the abilities of those on the autism spectrum. The Aczels favor job training that can be completed within four months. They created their own software testing curriculum based on protocols established by the International Software Qualifications Board. However, developing a custom curriculum is not necessary to start such an initiative. The Aczels point out that community colleges and vocational schools may have programs in place that prepare individuals for jobs within a short period of time.

Internships are an integral part of the TSG model. The organization looks for candidates who have earned college degrees (or come close) and have tried unsuccessfully to find employment. Some of the applicants chose college majors that offer limited employment opportunities, such as philosophy. Others were not able to sell themselves in interviews. Many come to TSG with no work experience of any kind to include on a résumé. In addition to providing job experience, the internships build self-esteem and self-confidence.

The mission of STEM Force Technology (www.stemforcetechnology.com) is to improve employment outcomes for young people interested in STEM careers. STEM is an acronym for the science, technology, engineering and math fields. The organization is based in Tempe, Arizona, which is home to many start-up technology companies.

Garret Westlake, PhD, founded the organization in 2011. He noticed increasing numbers of young people with Asperger's Syndrome who had skills and high grade point averages (GPAs) in college but could not find jobs. Westlake is also Assistant Dean of Students and Director of Disability Services at Arizona State University. "We've gotten better at helping young people transition to college," he says, "but they are not getting the career preparation they need."

Dr. Westlake works with local employers to place students in internships, and recent college graduates into jobs. The individuals are very high-functioning and possess skills that are in demand. He also runs a two-day Asperger's Leadership Academy for high school juniors and seniors to help them choose college majors that will give them marketable skills. In 2013, STEM Force Technology added a program to train individuals to perform software testing.

Dr. Westlake describes STEM Force Technology as a "social impact" company that works at the community level to create more inclusive workplaces. He stresses the need for parents to assume an active role within their own places of employment to develop internship and employment opportunities for autistic youth.

Not everyone with Asperger's Syndrome has the interest or aptitude to work in high technology. However, these models can be adapted to many different fields, such as the life sciences, finance and service businesses.

Green Bridge Growers (www.greenbridgegrowers.org) is an agricultural enterprise that uses aquaponics to grow produce year-round. Located in South Bend, Indiana, it was founded by Chris Tidmarsh, who is autistic, and his mother, Jan Pilarski. Its mission is to provide sustainable produce and create jobs for individuals on the autism spectrum.

Aquaponics is a technology where fish and vegetables are grown together. As Chris explains, "It's a highly productive, closed loop system. The fish fertilize the plants and the plants purify the water for the fish. It uses 90 percent less water than conventional farming and provides the competitive advantage of rapid harvests and four-season farming."

Green Bridge Growers launched using the Lean Startup business model. This means that they created a prototype to prove their concept, and now seek additional funding to grow and scale the business.

The prototype became operational in the summer of 2013. Green Bridge Growers currently sells produce to high-end restaurants and a local Whole Foods Market. Funding for the prototype was provided by a local non-profit that serves children and adults with disabilities. Local universities have provided advice and mentoring. As Jan says, it is a community-based social enterprise. They are now building a large-scale commercial greenhouse facility, which has been financed through crowdfunding and contributions from community supporters.

The impetus for the venture was Chris's difficulty managing in a traditional workplace. After graduating from college, he found a job researching and writing about environmental topics. Since he has a hard time processing and responding to verbal instructions, he requested that assignments be communicated via email. This proved difficult for the company, and the job did not work out.

Chris became interested in science and organic farming in college, where he earned degrees in chemistry, environmental studies and French. He participated in several farming internships. Aquaponics enables him to apply his passion for chemistry with his enjoyment of working outdoors and growing plants.

His mother Jan is a former community organizer, writer, project developer and college administrator and teacher. She recently turned her attention to urban farming, and along with Chris is a Master Gardener.

Chris and Jan emphasize that aquaponics is a STEM industry. The work involves many tasks that are repetitious and require precision, which are autistic strengths. Water chemistry must be monitored; plants must be seeded, watered, transplanted and harvested; and the growth of fish and produce must be measured.

To train its autistic employees, the organization uses visual materials such as step-by-step written instructions, check lists and photographs of the growing process. The training manual clearly explains the systems, patterns and repetition of tasks. Calendars and apps are used to remind workers of their duties.

As effective and necessary as these social enterprises are, it is critical that employers are educated on how to utilize the abilities of individuals on the autism spectrum. There is exciting evidence that this is happening, led by the international enterprise software company SAP AG.

In 2013, SAP set a goal that, by 2020, 1 percent of its workforce will be individuals on the autism spectrum. The organization is recruiting autistic workers in order to utilize the specialized skills they bring to the workplace. At the time of writing in the Spring of 2014, pilot programs have been implemented in Brazil, Germany, India and Ireland. Similar programs are now being launched in the United States and Canada.

Overseeing the autism initiative in the United States is Jose Velasco, himself the father of two young adults on the spectrum. He is quick to point out that this is not a charitable program. For SAP, it is an opportunity to utilize an untapped pool of creative, skilled workers who can help move the company forward. Like many organizations in the STEM space, SAP has trouble finding qualified candidates to fill open positions. According to Velasco, there are many individuals with autism who have the right credentials and aptitude to fill needs at SAP.

The organization is collaborating with Specialisterne, which provides specialized training for people on the spectrum, and the California Department of Rehabilitation (DOR), which helps fund the initial training. SAP submits open positions to the DOR that it believes match the capabilities of people with autism. The DOR and Specialisterne work in the recruitment process of qualified candidates, who are then screened at a workshop sponsored by SAP. Those who possess the right qualifications are then invited to participate in four weeks of training at the SAP offices.

The training is provided by Specialisterne and serves as an in-depth evaluation process in lieu of a traditional interview. It allows individuals to demonstrate their capabilities (rather than social savvy) and become familiar with SAP. Participants understand that they are job candidates and employment is not guaranteed.

In addition to hard skills, the training covers a variety of soft skills, such as how to work on a team, listen and follow instructions. During this period, the candidates have several opportunities to interact with their possible future managers. The managers also receive training on how to work with people on the autism spectrum.

A representative from a local non-profit called TransAccess shadowed the Specialisterne trainer. TransAccess provides transition and employment services to individuals with disabilities. It is a certified DOR vendor, and in the future will provide training to SAP job candidates.

New employees receive a variety of supports. They have access to the Specialisterne instructor. SAP provides mentors outside of the employee's work team who have an affinity for those on the autism spectrum. TransAccess provides an on-site job coach for the first 90 days of employment.

In addition to software development and testing, SAP is hiring workers with autism as technical documentation writers and business process analysts.

These organizations are sending a powerful message that autistic employees can be assets. I believe that such efforts will continue to grow, since so many people today know of someone who is on the autism spectrum. As a human resources director recently told me, "Five years ago, if you mentioned Asperger's Syndrome, I wouldn't know what you were talking about. Now, I can name several people who have it."

When I speak to employer groups, I stress that it is not necessary to create a large, enterprise-wide program. I know of companies that have partnered with local Asperger's / autism associations to create several internships, or to recruit qualified candidates to fill job openings. A common theme is that these efforts are initiated by an employee who is the parent of someone on the autism spectrum.

There are many things that employers can do to help Asperger's employees be productive and successful:

- Break training into short segments.

- Explain how tasks and assignments fit into the whole, and why particular steps or processes are important.

- Provide written instructions, outlines and check lists to augment verbal information.

- Make expectations specific and quantifiable (e.g. "30 entries or more must be made per hour").

- Avoid vague, abstract directives (e.g. "Take ownership of the project").

- Address any performance problems with clear, explicit language.

- Be mindful that what looks like a behavior or attitude problem is usually a communication problem.

- Assign a "work buddy" or mentor to explain social norms, encourage social interaction and answer questions.

- Relax standards for "teamwork" where possible, and allow the individual to focus on the technical aspects of the job.

- Take sensory processing problems seriously.

- Give an individual permission to take short breaks.

Specific workplace accommodations will be discussed in Chapter 8.

This is not to suggest that Aspergians do not need to develop their skills, or adapt to the norms of the workplace. However, when neurotypicals demonstrate flexibility and meet Aspergians half way, everyone wins.

Part II

COACHING STRATEGIES FOR GETTING AND KEEPING A JOB

Chapter 4

COACHING INDIVIDUALS WITH ASPERGER'S SYNDROME

THE EVOLUTION OF THE COACH

An apt analogy for the modern coach is a professional who assists individuals in negotiating the sometimes rough road between where they are and where they want to be.

The word "coach" has its origins in the fifteenth century in the Hungarian village of Kocs. There, the *kocsi szeker* ("wagon from Kocs") was born. Believed to be the first horse-drawn vehicle to utilize spring suspension, it provided a smooth, comfortable ride for passengers traversing rough, unpaved roads (Skedgell 2012). By the 1800s the word "coach" was used as slang at Oxford University to refer to a tutor who "carried" students through their exams (De Haan 2006).

Thomas Leonard is widely credited with developing the personal coaching profession in the late 1980s. A financial planner by trade, Leonard noticed that his clients often wanted more than financial advice. They wanted to know how to live more satisfying lives. When a client asked why there wasn't such a thing as a life coach, Leonard began researching the possibilities (Leonard n.d.). In 1992, Leonard founded Coach University to train and certify professional coaches. In 1994, he launched the International Coach Federation (ICF) (Leonard 2003).

Today, the ICF is an international professional association that accredits training programs, conducts research and produces industry conferences and publications. According to a study it sponsored, coaching is a multi-billion dollar, global industry (International Coach Federation 2012). There are many different types of coaching specialties: life coaches, wellness coaches, relationship coaches, business coaches and ADHD coaches to name a few. Organizations spend $1 billion per year on executive coaches to enhance the performance of senior managers (Dingfelder 2006).

A coach functions as a strategist, confidant and mentor who is focused on helping an individual reach his goals. Unlike psychotherapy, which addresses conflicts and problems from the past, coaching is about taking action and planning for the future. Coaching is also different than consulting. Rather than act as an expert who solves a client's problems, a coach helps a client find his own solutions and become more resourceful.

Coaching should not be confused with advice giving. Professional coaches are specifically trained *not* to give advice to their clients. People generally don't act on most of the advice they receive. This is because the advice reflects the needs, experiences and thought process of the giver.

Coaches use Socratic-like questioning to help clients think outside the box, consider options and find solutions that work for *them*. In *Quiet Leadership*, executive coach David Rock explains how each person's brain stores, organizes and retrieves information differently (Rock 2006, p.8). He writes, "Doing the thinking for other people is not just a waste of our own energy; it also gets in the way of other people working out the right answers" (p.9).

Imagine that I said, "You should only respond to emails at 9:00am and 3:00pm." You would almost certainly begin telling me why that schedule would not work. But what if I asked, "How can you better manage emails?" or, "Where do you need help prioritizing?" Those questions shift the focus to solutions that make sense to you. The same thing happens when suggestions are framed as open-ended questions: "What tasks can you delegate?" or "How valuable would it be to make a list of priorities for the week?"

I utilize coaching techniques but adapt them to the needs of individuals with Asperger's Syndrome. Later in this chapter, I describe how.

Although coaching is not psychotherapy, it draws on a number of therapeutic techniques, such as active listening, empathy, cognitive restructuring, reinforcement and reframing.

Carol Rogers' person-centered approach, which promotes "unconditional positive regard and acceptance" of clients (Peltier 2001, p.69), is particularly applicable when working with Aspergians. Many have had lifetimes of being bullied and ostracized. Often, neurotypicals are not aware of how hard individuals are trying to "fit in."

Imagine hearing, "You should know that," when you don't, and then being chastised for saying or doing the wrong thing! Or, being told that you are rude and not knowing why, or how to fix the problem. What would it do to your self-esteem to be fired from an entry-level job that is far below your intellectual capabilities and level of education?

When I acknowledge and validate the feelings and experiences of clients, they visibly relax. Some say that I am the only person to have done that. The conversation might go something like this:

"You thought that you were being helpful by correcting your co-worker's grammatical error," I say, "but she thought you were rude for pointing out a mistake in front of others."

"Exactly!" says the client, with a sigh of relief. "Wouldn't anyone want to know?"

Coaches use active listening skills to communicate that they have heard and understand what a client shares. These same skills can be taught to individuals with Asperger's Syndrome. Not all will master techniques such as reflecting and paraphrasing. But even basics such as nodding one's head or saying, "Uh-huh" to signal attention, will improve communication.

Alex read an article on the Internet about active listening. In typical Aspergian fashion, he interpreted "active" quite literally.

"Every time I try to actively listen, other people won't let me," he said.

I asked him to define active listening and give me two examples of when it didn't work. To Alex, *active* meant giving advice or sharing a story about his personal experience. He was surprised to learn that it refers to listening to comprehend what another person is communicating with their words, facial expression, tone of voice and gestures.

Alex started practicing listening to people with interrupting. Then he began noticing the more obvious nonverbal signals. Over several weeks his behavior became less intrusive.

Coaching is about action, not psychoanalysis. However, coaches may utilize aspects of Freud's psychodynamic view to help clients understand defenses and self-defeating behaviors (Peltier 2001, pp.24–25). Using Freud's theories as a basis, coaches try to get "inside the head" of individuals in order to make sense of their relationships, experiences and how they see the world. The psychodynamic approach includes all the theories in psychology that see human functioning based upon the interaction of drives and forces within the person, particularly unconscious, and between the different structures of the personality (McLeod 2007).

When I work with clients who are in corporate jobs, these concepts help them understand the behavior of others. For example, awareness of human defense mechanisms such as denial, rationalization and projection can explain office politics.

I pay close attention to parallel process (Peltier 2001, p.40) when I am coaching. This means that my reaction to a client mirrors how others react to that person. Aspergians typically have low awareness of how their behavior impacts others. When I find myself confused or frustrated by interactions during a coaching session, the clients' co-workers probably experience the same behaviors and have the same reaction.

The principles of CBT are widely applicable in coaching. It is empowering for a person to realize that the way he thinks about an event affects his emotions and behavior (Briers 2012, pp.5–6). A number of my clients have learned to challenge assumptions and limiting beliefs that were hurting their performance at work.

I have had success introducing the concept of cognitive distortions to high-functioning individuals. Dr. David Burns, a pioneer in the field of cognitive therapy, identifies ten common patterns of distorted thinking in his classic book, *Feeling Good: The New Mood Therapy* (Burns 1999, pp.42–43):

1. *All-or-nothing thinking*: seeing people and situations in absolute terms, such as good or bad, right or wrong, smart or stupid.

2. *Catastrophizing*: the tendency to exaggerate the potential for negative outcomes. Your boss points out one error in an assignment, and you decide that he's getting ready to fire you.

3. *"Shoulds"*: a strict set of rules about how people, including yourself, are supposed to act or do things, with exaggerated consequences if a rule is violated. Ellen thinks that colleagues should always meet deadlines, or be fired.

4. *Personalization*: assuming that you are the reason that someone behaved in a certain way, without considering other explanations: "Todd didn't say hello to me because he doesn't like me."

5. *Jumping to conclusions*: *mind reading*, where you conclude that someone is reacting negatively to you, without any evidence that this is true: "Dan didn't fix my computer because he wants my projects to be late"; or *fortune telling*, which is anticipating what could go wrong as an established fact: "The project will fail and I'll lose my job."

6. *Labeling*: assigning negative labels to yourself or other people without having evidence to support that conclusion: "My co-workers are selfish and unsupportive because they wouldn't cover for me"; or "The division head is an idiot for not giving me the promotion."

7. *Filtering*: paying attention only to negative information and filtering out positive information. Jill obsessed over one "needs improvement" in her performance review, and ignored the overall rating of "exceeds expectations" and the recommendation that she receive a raise.

8. *Disqualifying positives*: insisting that positive experiences don't count: "Anyone could have received the award."

9. *Emotional reasoning*: the belief that your *feelings* are the truth: "I feel stupid, so I must *be* stupid"; or "I'm worried about losing my job, so they must be ready to fire me."

10. *Overgeneralization*: global statements about one-time events. Because you entered one wrong formula into a spreadsheet, you believe that you're no good at budgeting. Or, you get off at the wrong subway stop and believe that you cannot use public transportation.

Cognitive distortions are hardly unique to individuals with Asperger's Syndrome. However, several characteristics of autism make them likely: anxiety, rigidity, difficulty understanding the motives and intentions of others, and chronic negative thinking.

Valerie Gaus, PhD, explains how she applies the CBT model in *Cognitive-Behavioral Therapy for Adult Asperger Syndrome* (2007). She writes:

> I have found that people with AS are vulnerable to any of the cognitive distortions, and like the general adult population, each patient makes his or her own unique combination of [thinking] errors. However, the one that is found in every patient with AS I have met is *all-or-nothing* thinking. (Gaus 2007, p.171)

My experience bears this out.

CBT can help individuals gain a more realistic perspective on events. For some, the realization that they can choose how to interpret and respond to situations makes it easier to cope in the workplace. Others have great difficulty grasping the concept of choice when it applies to their emotions.

Finally, coaching draws on the field of social psychology, which postulates that behavior is more strongly influenced by other people, and the context of a situation, than an individual's character (Peltier 2001, pp.136–137).

Social psychologists attempt to observe and understand behaviors by devising "real world" experiments and tests. The most famous example is Stanley Milgram's electric shock experiment. In the 1960s, Milgram, a psychologist at Yale University, set up an experiment where people were required to deliver electric shocks to students each time the student incorrectly answered a question. The voltage increased with each successive error.

The students were part of the experiment, and did not really receive any shocks. However, the participants in the experiment believed that they did. As the "voltage" increased, the students' reactions became more intense. They would plead to be released from the experiment. Participants who questioned the experiment and didn't want to deliver the punishment were convinced by the experimenter (an authority figure) to ignore the students' pleas and continue.

To everyone's surprise, 65 percent of the participants delivered the maximum shock (what they believed to be 450 volts) to the students. The results were used to illustrate how the social environment influenced otherwise non-violent individuals to follow the experimenter's directions (Cherry 2013).

Social psychology theories can help an individual understand the power of group dynamics, and how neurotypicals adjust their behavior based on social dynamics. They can build awareness of how an individual's behavior influences others, and the importance of observing cultural norms within the workplace.

This has been a brief description of some of the psychological theories used in coaching. To readers who want to learn more, I recommend *The Psychology of Executive Coaching, Theory and Application*, by Bruce Peltier (2001), and *Executive Coaching, Practices & Perspectives*, edited by Jennifer Garvey Berger and Catherine Fitzgerald (2002).

ADAPTING THE COACHING MODEL

Coaching offers customized, one-on-one support to assist individuals in reaching their goals. The process involves goal setting, identifying obstacles, brainstorming solutions and creating a workable action plan.

Neurotypicals and Aspergians alike benefit from the pragmatic nature of coaching. However, there are notable differences in the reasons they seek services, the nature of their obstacles and the type of interventions that will be successful.

Neurotypicals generally seek career coaching to enhance their productivity, increase their leadership ability or to explore vocational options that will bring greater satisfaction. When organizations sponsor coaching for employees, it is almost always offered as a benefit under the umbrella of professional development.

Individuals with Asperger's Syndrome seek coaching to address a problem. A person may be overwhelmed by the job search process, or have no idea of what jobs he is qualified to perform. He may struggle to sell himself at job interviews, confusing marketing one's skills with lying. An individual may have experienced multiple job losses and not know why. He wants to find work that is manageable.

Aspergians who have jobs may be concerned about a performance problem or disciplinary action. There may be conflicts with supervisors or co-workers. They may seek assistance to improve their general communication skills or learn how to manage time and projects efficiently. Some want to disclose their Asperger's Syndrome to their employer and request accommodations.

The role of the coach also differs. For neurotypicals, the coach serves as a facilitator. He asks the right questions so that clients find their own solutions. He helps them create compelling future visions, and challenge their fears and limited thinking. The process is about action, experimentation, learning and more action. Coaching sessions are fast-paced and usually last 30 minutes.

With Aspergians, the coach must assume a more directive role. These clients need skill development and how-to strategies much more than they need personal insight.

It is critical for the coach to be pragmatic. Abstract terms such as "leveraging strengths" and "defining core values" will have little meaning for these concrete, literal thinkers. I have clients in director-level jobs who are flummoxed by directives to "show leadership" or "think strategically." *How, exactly*, they wonder, *does one show leadership? What is an example of a strategic thought?*

Alicia came to me after working with a coach who did not have experience with Asperger's Syndrome. Alicia found many of the coach's suggestions confusing.

"She told me that there are goblins in my head that I need to get rid of," Alicia said.

I realized from my coaching training that Alicia was referring to "gremlins," which is coaching jargon for negative, limiting beliefs. Alicia confided to me that she was anxious about these gremlins, and asked whether they were actual entities in her brain. Alicia is a professional who earns over $100,000 per year. Despite her intellect, Asperger's Syndrome makes it difficult for her to understand abstract concepts.

An Aspergian client might have lost his job but not understand why. The coach must try to tease out what happened and teach the individual how to avoid a similar circumstance in the future.

Working with these clients takes time. Their narrative of events often requires clarification. The more loquacious individuals may provide great detail, either because they can't discern what information is relevant, or because they don't realize that others can infer meanings. The taciturn offer one- or two-word responses that must be painstakingly expanded. Clients with limited theory of mind may suddenly start talking about a person or technical aspects of their job that the coach would have no way of recognizing.

Professional coaches are taught to interrupt clients when they give too much detail, or launch into long stories about past events. The purpose is to keep sessions focused on strategies and action. I use this technique occasionally. My experience is that Aspergian clients need to explain events as they live them: by sharing the details.

I learn a lot when I listen without interrupting. How well can the individual see the gist of his situation? How does he perceive what is happening? Is his perception based on the relevant data? Does he become lost on tangents during his narrative? Are his reactions reasonable? What I see and hear in the coaching session is what interviewers, bosses and co-workers experience. This doesn't mean that I allow clients to ramble on and on. I do interrupt, sometimes. However, I do not rush clients or expect them to work at the pace of neurotypicals.

Coaching assignments usually require precise, detailed explanations. These individuals can become overwhelmed by too much new information, especially if it is verbal. I check to be sure that a session is not moving too quickly, and that the person doesn't have too much to do. Additionally, the majority of people I work with are learning new skills. It takes time for them to practice and participate in role plays. For these reasons, my coaching sessions last for one hour.

ASSESSING COACHING READINESS

In order for coaching to be effective, an individual must:

- *want* coaching

- devote time and energy to action steps

- be willing to try new things

- commit for a reasonable period of time.

The first point might seem superfluous. However, sometimes an individual begins coaching at the behest of a parent, spouse or other family member. These engagements don't go well, because the individual is not invested in the process. He shows up for sessions without an agenda. Assignments are completed in a cursory way, or not at all. He may resent having to come to the session.

A client and I spend part of every coaching session deciding what actions he will commit to taking in between our meetings. These actions are related to the achievement of his goals. I stress to an individual that he must be willing to devote time and energy to these action steps, or the coaching will not be effective.

My experience is that Aspergians who want coaching are diligent about following through with their assignments. When action steps are not completed, the problem usually is not low motivation. It may be:

- the steps were too big, or not specific enough

- the individual didn't know how to get started

- assignments were forgotten because they weren't written down

- specific days and times were not scheduled to work on assignments

- anxiety prevented the person from taking action.

Coaching is about change, which Aspergians don't like. It can be challenging to coax these clients to try something different. I learned this lesson early on.

Despite being experienced and qualified, Kelly was not being invited for interviews. Her résumé did not provide enough information about her abilities.

"All this entry says is that your title is Technical Documentation Writer, and that you write manuals and help screens," I said.

"Everyone knows what a technical writer does," Kelly said.

"The people who see this résumé might know what the job entails," I explained, "but they don't know about your technical expertise, the tools that you know how to use, or that you have done usability testing."

We discussed at length the concept of marketing one's skills on a résumé. Together, we came up with a list of Kelly's abilities and accomplishments. Her assignment was to rewrite her résumé, and bring a draft to our next session.

The next week, I reviewed Kelly's draft. It was an improvement, but there was much more to be done. Kelly wanted to discuss job search strategies. Concerned about consuming our time going over the résumé, I offered to edit the draft. Kelly agreed.

A few days later, I emailed a new version of the résumé to Kelly. At her next coaching session, Kelly thanked me and said that she had made some changes to the résumé I'd sent. After assuring her that this was expected, I asked to see the final product. I was shocked that it was almost exactly the same as the original. It was hard to stop myself from exclaiming, *"What did you do?!"*

I asked Kelly about her reticence to alter her résumé.

"I don't want to look like I am stuck up," she said.

Kelly also did not want to remove several part-time jobs she had during high school and college, even though they were unrelated to technical writing. To her, *all* work experience belonged on a résumé. "Otherwise, I am lying."

Finally, she explained, "I liked mine better."

The final step in assessing a person's coaching readiness is determining whether he will commit to it for a reasonable period of time. Individuals sometimes contact me thinking that three or four coaching sessions will transform life-long difficulties, or enable them to master new skills.

I set realistic expectations during the initial, exploratory meeting with a potential new client. I explain the importance of building momentum and reinforcing new skills and behavior. Ideally, a client has coaching sessions once or twice a week, at least in the beginning. I do not work with client less often than every other week. I have found that when too much time goes by in between meetings, clients become distracted and do not make progress.

Most coaching engagements last between three and nine months. Some clients continue longer, or resume coaching at a future time to address a new problem or situation. I ask new clients to make a three-session commitment, and then decide whether to continue. This is atypical in the coaching profession. Most clients are asked to make an initial commitment of three months of services. My experience is that people with Asperger's Syndrome need to try a few sessions to know whether coaching is effective. A single exploratory session is not enough to evaluate a person's readiness. My feeling is that there is no point in forcing a person to continue coaching for months if it is not working.

There are times during the exploratory session when it is clear that I cannot offer the type of assistance that a person needs. I am direct in saying so and try to make a referral.

About half of my clients also work with a psychotherapist or other mental health professional. Ordinarily this does not pose a problem, since coaching and psychotherapy are different services. However, if the client or I have concerns about his ability to take on the work of coaching, I arrange a consultation with his mental health provider.

THE COACHING MODEL

I use the following three-step coaching model with my clients:

1. Determine the person's goals.

2. Identify obstacles to reaching those goals.

3. Develop a realistic action plan.

Goal Setting

The coaching engagement begins by clarifying the individual's goals. I recommend to clients that they work on no more than three goals at a time. Sometimes the manageable number is one.

The goals of individuals with Asperger's Syndrome can be unexpected:

"Find a job I won't get fired from"... "Become less annoying"... "Learn not to be rude"... "Overcome my fear of talking on the telephone"... "Pass for neurotypical on a job interview"... "Not be weird"... "Read body language to know whether people are mad at me"... "Learn how to talk to people, so I'll be invited to lunch with my co-workers."

The goals may also be unrealistic, given an individual's abilities, education, experience or understanding of what it is possible to achieve.

Carl was in his 50s and married. Wanting a better paying job, his dream was to become an ice road trucker. He decided on this occupation after watching a television series about professionals who transport materials across frozen rivers and lakes in remote areas of Alaska and Canada. Despite the fact that he had no professional driving experience, and lived in a temperate region of the southern United States, Carl believed this was a viable option.

"What do you find attractive about the job, besides the potential for higher pay?" I asked.

"You're on the road for several weeks by yourself, and I like working alone," Carl said.

"What does your wife think of you being away for so long?"

"She won't mind," Carl replied confidently.

There are occasions when the initial goals change, or turn out not to be the real priority.

After eight years as a retail sales associate, Ben was bored. He wanted to find a career that was related to one of his many interests. These included astrology, numerology, yoga, cartology and hiking.

His initial career research was not promising. "Yoga teachers don't make much money, and I don't want to be in front of a crowd of people," he said. He discovered that astrologers and numerologists were mostly self-employed. "I need a steady pay check," he explained. Hiking also presented limited opportunities for employment and income. Cartology wouldn't work, because it would require another college degree and the field was competitive.

"Everything requires more schooling," Ben lamented.

"Usually people need to invest in some type of education or training to prepare for a new career," I said.

Deciding to try a different approach, I asked Ben what he liked about his current job. He described a number of positives. It was structured, and he knew exactly how to ring up sales. He knew the layout of the store, and could easily direct customers. His commute was short. He was friends with one of the other associates, and they often ate lunch together.

"Do you really want to find a new career," I asked, "or are you bored working in this particular store?"

Ben said it was the latter. Realizing the difficulty that Aspergians have adjusting to change, I suggested that Ben not look for a new job just yet. Instead, I recommended that he try to find an activity to enjoy in his free time, that would involve other people. He agreed to explore yoga classes and hiking groups.

I frequently employ the SMART model to help clients set realistic goals. The methodical, step-by-step format is well suited to people with Asperger's Syndrome.

SMART is an acronym for **S**pecific, **M**easurable, **A**chievable, **R**easonable and **T**ime-oriented. It works like this:

Step 1: State a specific goal (what does the client want, by when?).

Step 2: Decide how success will be measured.

Step 3: Determine whether the goal is achievable (does he have the skills, ability and resources needed to meet the objective?).

Step 4: Determine whether the goal is reasonable (the "reality check").

Step 5: Establish a time frame for achieving the goal.

Individuals often need assistance with this process, especially to answer questions three and four. A person may have limited awareness of his abilities, or the resources that will be needed to attain his goal. He may perseverate on an objective that is not achievable.

It is not a coach's role to judge an individual's goals. However, encouraging pursuit of the impossible (or highly improbable) will only create frustration. Rather than interject my opinion about whether a goal is achievable or reasonable, I let a client's research do the talking. Part of my job as a coach is to direct clients to resources that will provide the information they need to make good decisions. Finding their own answers helps them become more resourceful. It also prevents arguments. I often need to "connect the dots" for a client, so that he can focus on the right data, see options and set a realistic goal. But I do not tell a client what he should do.

There are individuals who reject *any* information that does not support their ideas. They insist on continuing actions that are not working, or on pursuing impossible goals. Experience can be the best teacher, even when it means failure. It may take several failed attempts before a person realizes that *he* needs to change.

Identify Obstacles

Once a client's goals are clear, the next step is to identify what is getting in the way of his achieving them. I find that this is usually a combination of two or three factors:

- *Need to learn new skills*: typically these relate to interpersonal communication or executive functions. They can also be job search specific, such as résumé writing or interviewing.

- *Need resources*: this includes information that will assist a client that he is not aware of. Examples are: assessments of abilities, interests and strengths; communication or organizational tools; or articles or Web sites.

- *Need for realistic action plan*: this refers to the actions that a client commits to taking in between the coaching sessions.

Realistic Action Plan

It is imperative that the coach make sure that action plans are specific, manageable for the individual and written down.

Aspergians tend to be perfectionists, and to have low tolerance of frustration. I explain that if certain actions do not work out, it simply means that we will need to re-strategize. Otherwise, a client might become very discouraged, or anxious that I will be upset with him. I stress that the assignments are for the benefit of the client, not the coach!

A client and I spend part of every coaching session debriefing his progress on assignments. When things go well, we move on to the next step. If there were problems, I try to identify what happened. Usually patterns emerge, such as an individual over-committing; having trouble managing time; not asking for help; giving up too quickly; or becoming mired in unimportant details. These patterns may need to be addressed first, in order for the primary goal to be achieved.

Sharon had lots of questions about every assignment. A simple self-assessment about her ideal work environment prompted a host of queries: What was the difference between an orderly and slow work pace? How could she be sure whether she needed a job with a lot of structure? If she wanted to do tasks by herself, but enjoyed being around people, was that a preference for working alone, or for daily interaction with others? Would minimal supervision make a job overwhelming? What if she preferred a low-stress job, but could tolerate more stress if she liked the work?

"You're having trouble with the assignments," I observed.

"I'm afraid to choose answers that might be wrong," she said.

Now in her 40s, Sharon had been fired from many different jobs. She wasn't sure why some of them didn't work out. The various assessments made her anxious, because she thought she was committing herself to whatever preferences she chose. She wanted to avoid choosing the wrong job again. We set the assessments aside. Instead, Sharon began reading about various career clusters, focusing only on whether the jobs sounded interesting. We also began to examine what had gone well in her previous jobs, including the skills and abilities she brought to employers.

TIPS FOR WORKING WITH INDIVIDUALS
Acknowledge and Validate Their Point of View

Like everyone else, people with Asperger's Syndrome want to be heard and understood. Listening intently to the individual, acknowledging his experiences and concerns, and validating his emotions are basic coaching skills that build rapport and trust. They are particularly important to members of this population, who are chronically misunderstood.

Megan, a customer service representative, received a warning for being rude to a customer. She was upset and anxious about possibly losing her job. The week before, her supervisor told her that she was taking too long to resolve customer calls. "I was afraid that the call was taking too long," she said. "I told the customer to hurry up because I only had three more minutes for the call."

"You were trying to follow the rules for resolving calls," I began. "So you let the customer know that you were under pressure to complete the call, and she thought you weren't doing your job."

"Yes!" she exclaimed, "I was trying to do what my boss wanted."

Once Megan felt heard, we could discuss why the customer reacted that way, and how to handle such situations in the future.

Be Curious

Seek to understand how these individuals perceive the world. I find that there is logic to their actions, no matter how odd those actions initially appear.

Although Kevin had a master's degree, he was having trouble finding a job. After two weeks of searching for openings, Kevin reported that he did not find any suitable jobs. This was puzzling, since he had skills that were in demand.

"Why don't we go through some of the job posts to see what employers are looking for?" I suggested.

Kevin agreed, and quickly passed by multiple opportunities that appeared to match his abilities. I asked him why he didn't want to apply.

"Those jobs all require a master's degree," Kevin said.

"I'm confused; you *have* a master's degree," I replied.

"I'm only responding to jobs that require an associate's," Kevin explained.

Kevin reasoned that jobs which required less than his current level of education would be "easy." He believed that an easy job would increase his chances for success.

I often ask clients to give me examples of what or how they did something. This helps me identify any knowledge gaps or confusion.

Laura was interested in changing careers and becoming a writer. She surprised me by announcing that she had already been responding to job openings. She had only performed the most basic of research into the occupation. It wasn't clear that she was even qualified for this work.

It turns out that Laura read an article that included job hunting statistics. It provided estimates of the average number of résumés that must be sent to get a job interview, and the average number of interviews required to get a job offer.

Laura created a mathematical formula to determine whether she was qualified to be a writer. If she responded to a certain number of jobs without being invited for an interview, it would mean that she did not have the necessary skills. Instead of looking at the big picture, Laura focused on data that were not relevant to her career change.

Frame Asperger's Syndrome as a Difference Not a Deficit

I explain to clients that their brains process information differently. There is nothing bad or wrong about this; it is just different. Many of my clients say that their self-esteem and self-confidence are low. I always feel a pang when a person asks me to show him how to be "normal." Discussing differences in how Aspergian and neurotypical brains work removes any blame or judgment of the individual.

Some clients are concerned that they are being asked to change who they are as individuals in order to get or keep a job. "I don't want to go through my life pretending to be neurotypical," one woman said. I explain that the goal of coaching is learning how to function within the neurotypical workplace, so that abilities can be utilized.

Be a Bridge to the Neurotypical World

I describe myself as someone who "translates" the actions and expectations of neurotypicals for clients.

When an individual describes behavior that would raise eyebrows (or worse), I explain how others would perceive it: "I understand that you were trying to be helpful, but a neurotypical would interpret a comment about her weight as rude." We discuss why this is so and what to do differently. Translating is another technique for avoiding blame or judgment of the client. It also encourages him to explore why others react to him in a negative way.

Point Out Patterns

I have had clients who have been on dozens of interviews, or lost a succession of jobs, yet they do not see a recurring pattern. Patterns highlight what needs to change. I might observe, "Getting interviews means that you are qualified for the jobs that you apply for. But you are not getting job offers. That means that you need to improve how you are communicating your abilities during an interview."

This technique is also useful when a person does not see how he is causing or contributing to a problem. Ed became quite defensive when colleagues complained about his brusque manner.

"I don't understand why they are upset," he said. "I am simply telling the truth."

"It is the way that you point out people's errors that they object to," I explained. "When you use statements like, 'It's simple if you pay attention,' or 'After working here this long it should be obvious,' other people feel belittled and judged."

"It's not my fault if they choose to think that," Ed replied. "Besides, not everyone at work is complaining about me."

"No, not *everyone* is complaining," I agreed. "But five or six people have gone to your boss about your behavior. That is a pattern."

Ed came back with several justifications, but finally acknowledged that he needed to change the way he spoke to his colleagues.

Be Specific and Direct

My rule of thumb is that what is obvious to me is probably not obvious to someone with Asperger's Syndrome. I know that hints and inferences will not be understood or acted upon, so I am concrete and direct. However, I am careful not to act in a patronizing way. Several clients have mentioned being insulted when service providers spoke to them as if they were children.

As a neurotypical, being specific and concrete is unnatural. Even after all these years of coaching Aspergians, there are still times when I am not precise enough.

Recently, I was helping Bill with his job search. He was in his late 40s and had worked at several different occupations. Even jobs that lasted for several years were very stressful. Typically, there were misunderstandings with a supervisor, or performance shortfalls. Bill wanted to explore occupations that would be enjoyable and manageable.

I gave Bill a template to help him organize his job research. It was keyed to the various sections of an online occupational database. I carefully explained how Bill could record his thoughts about various aspects of a job, such as primary tasks, work environment and educational requirements. I stressed that the purpose of this assignment was for Bill to record *his* thoughts, questions and concerns about different occupations.

Bill decided on four jobs to research. One of these was a government position that was not described in the occupational database. I sent Bill an article I found that described this job.

Bill brought the completed templates to his next coaching session, and we talked about what he discovered. When we got to the government job, Bill commented that it had taken him several hours to complete the form. The article was not in the same format as the database descriptions, and did not match the template. Bill spent a lot of time trying to fit information from the article into the fields on the template.

"I'm sorry," I said, "I should have explained that you did not have to follow the template exactly, or use it for every job."

"I wish you had told me," replied Bill, "because this took me a long time."

This is another example of the differences in how Aspergians process information. To Bill, the priority was not to record his impressions of various jobs. It was to record them in the template.

Jason was three weeks into his first job and he was having trouble adjusting to the formality of a business office. He had been reprimanded several times for being unprofessional. To Jason this was a vague term. "How do I act professional?" he asked me.

I was in the fortunate position of being able to speak with Jason's supervisor. One problem he mentioned was that Jason would run out of the office at the end of the day. Literally.

"I've told him that this is an office," his supervisor said.

"But did you specifically tell him to walk, not run, to the elevator?" I asked.

Later, when I related the conversation to Jason, he was surprised. "No one told me not to run," he said. "I don't want to be late for my train."

I am direct and matter-of-fact when addressing problem behavior.

"Running in the halls is disruptive and not acceptable in an office," I explained.

I do not make statements such as, "How could you not know that?" If the individual knew the action was wrong, he would not do it in the first place! Many of my clients are embarrassed to learn that they made a social gaffe.

Finally, the level of specificity and detail that is required will depend on the individual. Not everyone will need very detailed, step-by-step instructions. I ask what the person needs, and observe how well he completes tasks.

Explain Why

I notice consistently that when the purpose of a task or request isn't clear, an Aspergian will simply ignore it. Others may interpret this as disinterest, disrespect or insubordination.

A photocopier came between Jill and her colleagues. Jill worked in a medical office, and was told several times to use a particular machine. To Jill this was illogical because there was another copier much closer to her desk. Rather than comply, or find out why the request was made, Jill continued to use the wrong copier.

"Your colleagues have referred to the copier they want you to use as 'our machine,'" I said. "This tells me that it is specifically for people in your department."

At my urging, Jill asked a co-worker why she couldn't use the other copier. It turned out that the machine near her desk was for nurse practitioners, who needed ready access to stay on schedule with their patients.

"Why didn't anyone tell me that before?" Jill asked. She never used the nurses' machine again.

Break Tasks into Small, Specific Steps

Asking an individual to "update your résumé," or "make a project check list" is too general. To follow such instructions, a person needs to see the big picture first. Neurotypicals would start with the concept of a résumé, and then fill in the details: summarize my skills and experience, provide contact information, an objective, descriptions of previous positions, education.

People on the autism spectrum do the opposite: they think in terms of details first, and then fit the details together to see the whole. This can make it hard to know what the end point is, what information is relevant, what all of the steps are and how to begin.

I find it helpful to state the big picture (context) and then walk an individual through the specific steps. "The purpose of the check list is to remind you of everything you need to do to enter customer information into the database. What's the first thing you do to start a new record?"

Be Pragmatic

It is important to avoid abstract concepts and terms. An Aspergian may not be able to respond to a question like, "What will it look like when you find the right career?" Instead, I ask "What is important to you in a job?" and provide a list of examples.

Overly optimistic statements such as, "You can be anything!" should be avoided. An Aspergian will take that literally and disregard all evidence to the contrary. I talk instead about finding a good match, the right type of work environment or a job that will emphasize areas of ability rather than limitations.

Frame Change as an Experiment

It is less intimidating this way. Without a qualifier, a person might worry that he will have to continue using a technique even if it is not working. Experimenting also encourages a more flexible mindset.

Usually, the time period for the experiment is one or two weeks. I might ask a client to chart or log their results, and email me with a daily progress report.

We set benchmarks to evaluate whether the change is working. Otherwise, to perfectionist Aspergians it might be considered a failure if miraculous results don't happen in 7 or 14 days. I also prepare individuals to expect some discomfort at first.

When I know the person's source of motivation, it can be used as the impetus for change. Mike, for example, wanted a girlfriend.

"I need a job so that I can get my own place," he explained. "I can't tell a girl that I still live with my parents."

This was useful information when his job search was flagging. "What can you do this week to find a job, so you can get your apartment and girlfriend?" I asked.

Sometimes, even an extreme consequence such as job loss fails to override the Aspergian resistance to change. Eileen was a nurse whose lengthy patient notes made it increasingly difficult to manage her case load. Yet, she balked at a colleague's suggestions to include less detail.

"I'm confused," I said. "The other nurse has worked at the clinic for several years, and says that your notes contain much more information than is necessary. It sounds like briefer notes would help you keep up."

"I know," Eileen said, and paused. "But I *like* my way."

IS IT RESISTANCE OR ASPERGER'S SYNDROME?

Sometimes what appears to be resistance is really a feature of Asperger's Syndrome. Not recognizing this can cause tension and mistrust, particularly when it appears that the individual is not trying or doesn't care.

Be aware of these signs that may *not* be resistance:

Not Following Through on Assignments

The problem might be action steps that are too big, or not spelled out clearly, or anxiety. Ask the person to describe what got in his way: "You sat down to research careers, and then what happened?" If he says that he doesn't know, offer some educated guesses. The individual may not realize what went wrong, or how to articulate it, or he may be embarrassed.

These are learning opportunities. I often "connect the dots" for individuals who have trouble seeing cause–effect relationships. I will observe that assignments are forgotten when they are not written down. Or, that a client doesn't get around to tasks unless they are specifically scheduled.

Open-ended questions can be used to prompt the individual to solve problems. "How will you remind yourself to update your résumé?" Or, "Relying on your electronic organizer isn't working. What else can you try?" If he is not able to come up with an alternative solution, make a suggestion. "Here's a technique that many people find to be effective…"

Appears Disinterested or Disengaged

It is not pleasant to sit opposite a client who is slumping in his chair, staring at the floor or out of the window or speaking in a monotone. Ditto when the answer to every question is, "I don't know," or another three-word sentence.

The individual may literally not know what to say in response to a question. Or, if he is interrupted when formulating an answer (e.g. "Did you hear me?"), he may forget what he wanted to say. Problems with dual tracking processing could mean that he is unable to look someone in the eye *and* listen to what they are saying.

Some Aspergians have little awareness of their body language, and send unintended messages with their facial expressions, gestures or tone of voice. The intention to make eye contact could result in an unnerving stare. The person may look or sound angry when he is not.

Always inquire rather than assume. I might say, "You're not looking at me, and I'm not sure what that means."

Interrupting

This behavior is common among Aspergians and usually has nothing to do with bad manners. If the individual has poor short-term memory, he may interrupt to make his point before he forgets. If he has trouble processing auditory information, particularly during group conversations, he may interject before he loses track of the conversational thread.

Quite a few clients tell me that they cannot tell when other people are finished speaking. They do not pick up on the rhythm of conversation, or catch the subtle variation in vocal tone when a speaker finishes a sentence. Neurotypicals register these cues subconsciously.

Even so, interrupting has negative consequences during interviews and at work. Some individuals find it helpful to develop the habit of pausing for two seconds before they speak.

Rejects Every Suggestion

This could simply be resistance to change. Or, it could be something else.

Depression due to repeated failures, social isolation, under-employment and other stresses can lead to a feeling of helplessness. The person may not believe that change is possible, or not have the energy to follow through on strategies. A referral to a psychotherapist might be indicated.

Past experiences may be interpreted as absolutes. Clients have recalled failed job interviews or a workplace conflict from 15 years ago as evidence that their circumstances cannot improve.

The individual may believe that his original solution was the one correct response. Or, he is perseverating on everything that can go wrong. Ask why the person believes that a suggestion will not work. If he says that he has already tried it, find out when and under what circumstances.

Will was eager to work for a particular employer. I encouraged him to look at the company's Web site for job openings.

"I did that already," he said. "There are no jobs."

"When was the last time you checked?" I asked.

"Three years ago," he said.

Anxiety can certainly be a factor. The individual may not want to admit being nervous about talking on the telephone or being around strangers.

Chapter 5

FINDING THE RIGHT JOB

Over the past three years, there has been a significant increase in the number of young people in my practice. Many of these job seekers have college degrees, yet struggle to find work. Some believe that having a degree guarantees employment. They plan on sending out a few résumés, going on three or four interviews and choosing among the job offers!

I also work with older adults who have spent years trying to find the right job match. Some are in jobs that emphasize their areas of challenge, and want to find something less stressful. Others endure one job loss after another. Still others are under-employed in occupations that do not utilize their intellect or level of education.

Thorough occupational research is important for anyone, but it is critical for individuals with Asperger's Syndrome. Based on my experience, these are the most common mistakes individuals make when choosing a job or career:

- *Basing decisions only on interests*: interest in a subject should not be confused with having the ability to make a living in the field. I suggest that individuals research the actual jobs that are available, including the primary tasks and skills needed to complete those tasks. This should be done before investing time, money and effort in post-secondary education.

- *Not considering the work environment*: it is my experience that work environment is as important, or even more important, than job tasks for people with Asperger's Syndrome. Jobs that require a significant amount of multitasking, speed and sophisticated levels of interpersonal communication will be difficult or impossible to manage. (Work environment is discussed in detail later in this chapter.)

- *Not looking at options*: because of a tendency toward one-track thinking, individuals may not consider jobs that are a better match for their aptitudes and abilities. Those with limited insight into their capabilities may embark on a frustrating quest to obtain jobs for which they are not qualified.

- *Choosing college majors without researching the job market*: although it may not be possible to predict a job market years into the future, one can usually make good predictions based on economic trends. Competitive fields with few job openings will require a level of networking that is unrealistic for many Aspergians. They often cannot compete with more socially savvy job candidates. Individuals who obtain liberal arts degrees may discover that an advanced degree is necessary to work in a certain field.

- *Rushing*: young people with Asperger's Syndrome may not be ready for full-time, post-secondary education directly after high school. In *The Complete Guide to Asperger's Syndrome*, Tony Attwood cites research that supports his observation that, "the emotional maturity of children with Asperger's syndrome is usually at least three years behind that of their peers..." (2007, p.131). I observe this to be true of many young people I coach. There is a distinctly adolescent quality to individuals in their early to mid-20s. I believe that most need time after high school to mature and "catch up" to their neurotypical peers.

    This is why it can be beneficial for a person to work part-time and/or take a class or two at a community college after graduating high school. Attending college full-time, particularly if this involves moving away from home and living on a campus, can be completely overwhelming for Aspergians.

A four-year college degree is not right for everyone, nor is it the only path to gainful employment. Vocational or other post-secondary education that provides training for specific jobs is a viable option for many individuals. More and more community colleges are offering programs that prepare students for the many mid-level jobs that do not require a four-year degree.

Based on my experience, individuals with liberal arts degrees tend to struggle to identify manageable jobs and to compete with other job seekers.

GOOD JOBS FOR INDIVIDUALS WITH ASPERGER'S SYNDROME

Parents and professionals often ask me what jobs are best for people with Asperger's Syndrome. They hope that I can produce a list of occupations that will guarantee employment success.

Unfortunately, it is not possible to create such a list, because Aspergians vary so widely in their abilities, challenges and need of support. I have coached people in all kinds of job and careers. Here are some examples:

accountant • administrative assistant • analyst • bus driver • chemist • claims processor • college professor • computer programmer • consultant • creative writer • customer service representative • data entry clerk • editor • electrician • engineer • fine artist • geographic information system (GIS) technician • graphic artist • grocery bagger • laboratory technician • lawyer • librarian • meteorologist • nurse • paralegal • personal assistant • physician • physicist • political canvasser • production manager • records manager • reporter • retail sales associate • sales manager • screenwriter • sound technician • supply chain manager • teacher (adult education) • teacher (early childhood) • technical documentation writer • veterinarian • warehouse worker • web developer.

When I am working with a client to determine manageable occupations, we look at four areas:

1. interests

2. talents and skills

3. right work environment

4. impact of Asperger's Syndrome.

I consider each of these to be important pieces of a puzzle. All of them must fit together in order to identify occupations with the greatest likelihood of success.

Interests

An individual's interests are the logical place to begin occupational exploration. Most people want work that is at least somewhat engaging.

Sometimes I work with a person who has no idea what type of work he would like. More commonly, clients have limited interests, too many interests or interests that are unrealistic given their abilities, education or geographic region.

One man wanted to be a computer technician, but only to fix certain models of computers.

A woman with aspirations in the entertainment field didn't want to move from her small town in the Midwest. A young sports enthusiast set his sights on a broadcasting career, despite having a serious speech impediment.

As discussed in Chapter 1, many Aspergians have at least one "special interest" that is pursued with unusual intensity. The individual develops an encyclopedic knowledge of whatever topic has captured his interest. Luke was passionate about World War II weaponry. He was not at all versed in the politics of the war, the gross magnitude of human suffering or how it shaped history. However, he could rattle off all sorts of facts about Thompson submachine guns, Winchester shotguns, and various bazookas, flame throwers, hand grenades and bayonets.

Special interests can lead to fulfilling careers for individuals on the autism spectrum. Temple Grandin is a well known example. A childhood visit to her aunt's Arizona ranch sparked an interest in cattle and cattle chutes (Grandin 2006, p.109). She went on to earn a doctorate in animal science and developed a very successful career designing humane livestock facilities. Almost half of the cattle in North America are handled in systems she designed.

However, it is a mistake to assume that interests, special or otherwise, will always lead to gainful employment.

Several years ago, I participated in training for vocational rehabilitation specialists. One of the counselors was working with a client whose goal was to be an airline pilot. It was the only career that this man envisioned for himself.

Since this client had no aviation background, the vocational counselor questioned him to learn more about his interest. The client wanted to be an airline pilot so that he could wear a uniform!

I often repeat this story because it is an excellent example of how restricted interests in autism can negatively impact a job search. This man focused on a single—and in this case, irrelevant—detail about commercial aviation. He had no concept of what it means to be an airline pilot, or understanding that it was a completely unrealistic career choice.

This story does have a happy ending. The counselor found his client a job as a doorman at an upscale hotel. The man was completely satisfied because each day he wore a uniform.

PROBE INTERESTS!

I say to clients, "It's great that you want to be [*insert occupation*]. What do you see yourself doing once you are working in the field?"

The answer I receive most often is: "I don't know; I haven't thought about it."

This is a troubling response because it sets an individual up for a lot of potential frustration. It is true that many people do not work in jobs related to their post-secondary schooling. However, Aspergians are less adaptable than neurotypicals. They begin with a smaller pool of suitable jobs to choose from.

Alec is typical of many history majors I've coached. After discovering how very few job opportunities there were at museums, he decided to pursue archivism. He pictured himself spending his days absorbed in examining and categorizing historic photographs and documents.

A bit of research revealed that archivists spend a lot of their time creating and maintaining electronic databases. Alec did not have strong computer or database skills, and was not particularly interested in learning them.

There are also practical concerns, such as whether the individual can complete the required education, and compete for jobs in more competitive fields.

Steven earned a bachelor's degree in political science with the goal of finding a job in public policy. He figured that his knowledge of government, interest in research and 3.8 GPA would make it easy to find an entry-level position.

Instead, Steven found himself in a field that attracted many applicants and offered a small number of jobs. Employers expected job applicants to have internships or related volunteer experience. Steven had neither. During the school year, all his energy was devoted to keeping up with class work. He had not been able to find any internships during summer breaks. Most of the job openings were in the Washington, DC area, and Steven did not want to move.

Steven continued to visit job boards, send out résumés and hope for interviews. But now, 11 months after graduation, he wasn't thinking about shaping public policy. His priority, and that of his parents, was *any* job that would provide steady income.

An interest inventory is a helpful tool for individuals who are confused about their direction, too limited in their thinking, or who have too many interests. These assessments ask a person to rate his interest in various subjects or activities. Based on his responses, a list of possible jobs is generated. An interest inventory does not measure whether a person has the aptitude or skill to succeed in an occupation. It suggests vocational possibilities based on interests.

Interest inventories are widely available. Some can only be administered by a qualified career counselor. Others are available to individuals via the Internet at low or no cost. The quality of interest inventories varies. I suggest using assessments that have been scientifically validated to measure what they claim to.

Interest Inventories and Asperger's Syndrome

There are caveats when administering an interest inventory to someone with Asperger's Syndrome.

They have trouble imagining what they haven't actually experienced. An individual may not know how to rate items that are novel or too abstract. One young man asked, "What exactly does it mean to 'care for others'?" Differentiating "strongly liking" an activity from "liking" or "somewhat liking" can also be challenging.

Such confusion can skew results. For a while, I used an interest inventory that asked individuals to rate over 150 items. Some clients evaluated nearly every item as "neutral" (neither liking nor disliking the subject or activity) or as something they disliked. One or two items were given very high interest ratings. The assessment indicated strong interest in a certain career cluster based on only one or two responses.

I have experienced similar problems with assessments that ask individuals to indicate whether they would enjoy performing a task, *regardless of whether they know how to do it*. I knew I was in trouble when one young person asked, "What is a blueprint?" A package of those assessments is collecting dust in one of my filing cabinets. The questions are too abstract for my clients.

My experience with the Self-Directed Search® (SDS) has been positive. It is based on the work of psychologist John Holland. According to Holland's theory, there are six basic occupational personality styles and corresponding work environments (Eikleberry 2007, p.7). Holland believed that people are happiest when their work environment matches their personality style.

The six Holland types are: Realistic, Investigative, Artistic, Social, Enterprising and Conventional. They are referred to as RIASEC (*"ray-sec"*). What follows is a brief description of each type, based on *The Career Guide for Creative and Unconventional People* (Eikleberry 2007, pp.9–12).

Realistic types prefer to work with things and use their hands. They are often mechanically inclined and enjoy being outdoors. The skilled trades and agriculture are examples of occupations that appeal to this type.

Investigative individuals enjoy learning how things work and solving problems. They are analytic and task-oriented. Jobs in science, technology and mathematics appeal to these types, who show a preference for intellectual pursuits.

Both the Realistic and Investigative types prefer working alone; the former with things and the latter with ideas.

Artistic types value self-expression and original ideas. They thrive in unstructured environments where they are free to create. They are usually talented in art, music, drama or writing. Careers in this cluster include the fine arts, as well as commercial occupations such as Web site design and journalism.

Social types want to help others. This may be through direct service, such as counseling, healing or teaching, or in the development of a program or process that benefits others.

Enterprising individuals enjoy taking risks and managing other people. They want to direct, influence and persuade others. Attractive occupations involve leadership, sales or entrepreneurship.

Conventional types prefer routine work and established procedures. They often possess mathematical and clerical skills and enjoy organizing information. Administrative, banking and accounting are examples of Conventional jobs.

The SDS generates a three-letter summary code based an individual's top scores. The code RCS means that a person's highest interest matches Realistic occupations, his second highest matches Conventional and his third highest matches Social. The accompanying report suggests occupations based on various combinations of the summary code (e.g. RCS, RSC and SRC).

The results of the assessment almost always make sense to my client, and to me, based on what I know about that person. The correlation to work environment is important, since this is a crucial component of workplace success for people with Asperger's Syndrome. The characteristics of each type are straightforward and easy to grasp.

It may surprise you to know that a fairly large number of my clients show a Social preference. Even though they have difficulty with interpersonal interaction, they want work that benefits others in some way.

Realistic and Investigative preferences are common, which makes sense for these concrete thinkers. The Artistic preference also shows up often, and I know of many Aspergians who excel at writing, art and photography.

I pay particular attention to a very strong Conventional score. It is common for Aspergians to need structured jobs with clear parameters and well-defined end points. Many cannot cope with novel situations or complex problem solving. When structure and routine are priorities, the number of potential occupations narrows considerably. One would not make this determination based solely on the SDS score. However, a strong Conventional preference should be noted.

Usually when I combine a client's career interests with their top choices from the interest inventory, we will have a list of between five to ten possibilities. At this point in the coaching process, I do not worry whether the jobs are realistic. The goal is exploration.

Talents and Skills

The terms *talents* and *skills* are often used interchangeably, however, I make the distinction with my clients. I want them to understand the difference between their natural abilities, and proficiencies that they can learn and develop over time. For example, an Aspergian may dismiss an occupation because he does not currently possess the needed skills or experience. Additionally, job search skills such as résumé writing, networking and interviewing can seem overwhelming. When I explain that these are skills that everyone has to learn and practice, the process becomes less intimidating.

I give clients a list of common talents and skills and ask them to indicate which they possess. Not everyone is able to complete this independently.

When an individual's abilities are not clear, I will suggest an aptitude assessment. Typically, an individual takes a series of timed tests that measure various abilities such as verbal reasoning, mechanical or numeric ability, or spatial relations. Based on the results, occupational areas where there is the greatest likelihood of success are suggested. These assessments cannot predict the right job, but they can provide guidance. It is probable, for instance, that someone with poor numeric ability will not do well in accounting.

Brian enthusiastically described his love of numbers. He had many challenges, and worked extremely hard for four years to earn an associate's degree. According to an aptitude assessment, his numeric ability was low. He could not recall which mathematics classes he took in college. He was puzzled when I asked whether he enjoyed statistics. Finally, I asked him to add six plus five. He had to write down the equation to solve it.

Brian did indeed love numbers. He loved to look at them, draw them and find interesting patterns in them. "In a few weeks," he told me excitedly, "it's going to be 10–11–12!" He was referring to the date: October 11, 2012.

In contrast, Eric showed a very strong aptitude in spatial relationships. When I explained what that meant his eyes lit up. "I've always enjoyed taking things apart, seeing how they work and putting them back together!"

This was surprising since Eric was researching administrative jobs. When I asked him about the discrepancy he said, "I didn't know what kind of job I could do that involves taking things apart, but I know that I can sit behind a computer."

Although it is not a career tool, an up-to-date neuropsychological evaluation can provide valuable information related to occupational choices. Clinical neuropsychologists conduct interviews and various tests to understand an individual's brain functioning. They evaluate cognitive ability in areas such as attention, memory, language, visual-spatial ability and executive functioning. The evaluation is used to diagnose a variety of disorders, including autism.

Clinicians summarize test results and their observations in patient reports that are written in lay person's language. Evaluations of adults include vocational recommendations.

This information is helpful for understanding how a person's strengths and weaknesses could impact employment. Someone with poor working memory, for example, will have difficulty in jobs that require multitasking.

Sarah was a client who had been diagnosed with NLD. Despite having a college degree, she had been fired from six jobs. The problem was usually that she couldn't learn jobs quickly enough. She had many challenges, including marked impairment in visual discrimination and visual memory.

To earn some money, she took a job handing out food samples in a grocery store. This would seem to be an easy job for a college graduate. However, it took Sarah an inordinate amount of time to set up her display table each morning. One reason was that she couldn't easily locate products on the store shelves. She had to painstakingly scan rows of items three and four times to find the product she needed to hand out that day. It was a slow and painful process of matching a product name and logo to a photograph on her instruction sheet.

She also had problems figuring out how to set up and use the toasters, blenders and warmers that were used to prepare the samples.

Each morning, Sarah wondered anxiously whether her supervisor would check in during her set up, and realize how long it took.

By understanding Sarah's cognitive strengths and challenges, we were able to explore better options and, in a few months, she found a less stressful job.

Neuropsychological testing does have limitations. Tests are administered in a controlled setting, free of the distractions of the workplace. Clients sometimes tell me that the pressure of reacting in "real time" at work causes them to have trouble performing tasks that according to their evaluation should be "easy."

Work Environment

It bears repeating that work environment can be as important, or even more important, than job tasks for individuals on the autism spectrum. Factors to consider include aspects of the physical surroundings, the demand for interpersonal interaction and productivity requirements.

Physical	Interpersonal	Productivity

• Location: cubicle, printing plant, construction site
 	
• Sensory: noise level, odors, visual distractions, tactile sensations
 	
• Task performance: visuo-motor coordination, visual detail, fine and gross motor skills
	• Type of interaction:
	
	   ◦ Scripted and routine or novel and complex
	
	   ◦ Co-workers or customers
	
	• Company culture: collegial, hierarchical, pressured, etc.
		• Pace of job
		
		• Amount of structure
		
		• Level of independence
		
		• Decision making and problem solving
		
		• Multitasking
		
		• Big picture or details

Problems with the physical workspace are largely sensory-based. An individual might find certain occupations to be off limits because of sensitivity to:

- *odors*: printing plant, restaurant, cosmetics department

- *noises*: construction site, cubicle, factory

- *visual distractions*: fluorescent lighting, flashing lights

- *tactile sensations*: tight-fitting uniforms, hats, formal attire (e.g. neck tie).

He might become quite anxious when surrounded by people, such as at a call center or event stadium. Noisy environments or those that require working in groups might best be avoided, if a person has trouble processing auditory information.

The performance of certain tasks might be impacted by poor hand–eye coordination or fine motor control. Examples are assembly work or stuffing envelopes at a mailing facility.

Requirements for interpersonal communication can be difficult to evaluate, yet they factor heavily into employment success. It is useful to think in terms of how *sophisticated* a level of interaction is required. Some individuals manage quite well when interaction is limited to persons within their department or work group. Jobs that are tightly scripted, like some telemarketing positions, are also possibilities.

Others can handle more complex exchanges, such as those involving customers. Very high-functioning Aspergians can succeed in jobs that involve working with colleagues in different parts of the organization, or with vendors and customers.

As a rule, Aspergians do not perform well in competitive environments where there is pressure to produce. Many say that they need supportive bosses and co-workers. They can be quite attuned to the emotional state of those they work with. Some become agitated in environments where there is tension, hostility and aggression.

Aspergians tend to be slow, methodical workers. This is not always the case. Jim fixes recycled cell phones. He works so quickly that his employer has trouble keeping him busy.

However, it is not uncommon for individuals to have trouble meeting productivity standards.

The challenge is to know the abilities of the individual, and match them to the:

- pace of job

- amount of structure

- level of independence required

- complexity of decision making and problem solving

- amount of multitasking

- need to see the big picture.

Sometimes all that is needed is patience on the part of an employer. A longer training period, written instructions and opportunities to practice a process can pay off in a loyal, long-term, productive employee.

Richard's first job task was to scan documents. An administrative assistant was given the job of training him. Richard could not remember the multiple steps, which the assistant explained to him verbally. As the morning wore on, Richard could tell that she was becoming annoyed by his repeated questions. At one point, she commented that the job should not be so difficult.

Richard's anxiety rose and, predictably, so did the number of mistakes. When he returned from lunch, he was told that the manager wanted to see him.

The manager was an older woman who I'll guess sensed that Richard needed extra help. She slowly and patiently showed him the procedure, and suggested that he take notes. The last I heard, he had been at the job for six months and was doing well.

Important Job Criteria & Ideal Work Environment (Worksheet 5.1) is a self-assessment that asks individuals to identify aspects of work that are crucial for their success. Questions range from the very basic (salary, commuting distance) to the level of supervision needed and preferred amount of interaction with others. This assessment can be used to help narrow down occupational choices. It can also reveal unrealistic expectations on the part of an individual.

I pay particular attention to how a client answers question 7 (How much structure do you need in a job?) and question 8 (What kind of pace do you prefer?).

As discussed earlier in this chapter, individuals who say that they need a lot of structure—to know exactly what to do and when—probably need jobs that involve executing routine tasks. Knowing this rules out occupations that require independent decision making and complex problem solving.

The pace at which a person is expected to work is important for obvious reasons. One woman planned to apply for a job in a restaurant despite saying that she wanted a slow and steady work pace.

"I'm picturing a restaurant at lunch or dinner time," I said, "with lots of hungry people being served meals at the same time. I see that as a hectic environment where you have to move fast."

She agreed that a restaurant would not be a good choice.

Worksheet 5.1

IMPORTANT JOB CRITERIA AND IDEAL WORK ENVIRONMENT

1. How many hours do you want to work per week?

   _____

2. What is your maximum commute (time and distance)?

   _____

3. How will you get to and from work? ☐ Drive my own automobile
   ☐ Get a ride from someone else ☐ Use public transportation ☐ Walk

4. How much money do you want/need to make? _____
   ☐ per hour ☐ per week ☐ per year

5. Are you willing/able to obtain further training to qualify for a particular job? ☐ Yes ☐ No

6. Do you prefer to: ☐ perform the same duties every day
   ☐ perform different duties every day ☐ perform a combination of new and routine duties

7. How much structure do you need in a job? ☐ A lot: I need to know *exactly* what to do and when ☐ Some: I need direction in terms of tasks and priorities, *and* flexibility to plan how and when I perform my duties ☐ Little: I need to plan my schedule independently, based on my judgment

8. What kind of pace do you prefer? ☐ Fast pace; tight deadlines don't bother me ☐ Relaxed: there are deadlines, but they are not urgent ☐ Slow and steady

9. How do you prefer to work? ☐ Alone ☐ Minimal interaction with others ☐ Daily interaction with others ☐ Lots of interaction with others

10. How much supervision do you need? ☐ Close supervision and lots of direction ☐ Regular supervision (daily check-ins) ☐ Minimal supervision and direction ☐ No supervision (self-employment)

11. Do you want to work: ☐ Indoors   ☐ Outdoors

12. Do you prefer a work environment that is: ☐ Formal   ☐ Informal

13. Are you better at: ☐ Analytic, linear problem solving   ☐ Intuitive, big picture thinking

14. Do you prefer: ☐ Detailed, well-defined work   ☐ Creative or strategic work

15. Do you prefer working with (check all that apply):   ☐ Facts and information   ☐ Ideas   ☐ Numbers   ☐ Your hands   ☐ People ☐ Animals

16. Check the characteristics that are very important for you to have in a job:

☐ Challenges my intellect   ☐ Involves some risk   ☐ Includes travel ☐ Utilizes my creativity   ☐ Helps others   ☐ Allows me to express my ideas   ☐ Work that I like   ☐ Lots of opportunity for advancement ☐ Good benefits ☐ Lots of vacation time ☐ Being needed ☐ Job security   ☐ Low stress   ☐ Low responsibility

17. What other criteria are important to you?

_____

18. What criteria are you willing to compromise on in order to find a job that you like, in the shortest amount of time possible?

_____

_____

A WORD ABOUT TEAMWORK, PEOPLE SKILLS AND MULTITASKING

Ability to work on a team, good people skills, and the *ability to multitask* are ubiquitous job requirements. Literal-minded Aspergians may disqualify themselves from jobs that would be a good match. "I know my people skills aren't good," they say.

I explain that these are not absolute terms, and can mean very different things depending on an industry, the type of job and even a particular company. People skills are much more important for a retail sales associate than for a computer programmer. The amount of multitasking required of someone working in my town library, which serves 6000 residents, will be significantly less than for a person who works at the Boston Public Library.

Do not assume that an individual will make these connections. Help him to imagine what a work setting will be like and the type of interactions or level of multitasking there will be.

Over the years my clients have been remarkably consistent in describing work environments that are conducive to their success:

- minimal interruptions during the day

- limited amount of multitasking (rapid attention shifting)

- ability to complete one task before beginning another

- relaxed pace without urgent deadlines

- structured job with clearly defined duties

- some elements of routine

- explicit instructions (examples, priorities, how to get started)

- quantifiable performance expectations

- supportive supervisor and co-workers

- quiet workspace that is free of strong odors, bright lights and loud sounds.

Impact of Asperger's Syndrome

I believe that the more an individual understands about how Asperger's Syndrome impacts him, the easier it will be to find a manageable job.

Some individuals are deeply troubled to be told that they are on the autism spectrum. They challenge the diagnosis, and tell me about all of the symptoms that do not match. Those who attend Asperger's events or support groups may be very uncomfortable to be around people who are more significantly impacted.

The majority of my clients say that they are relieved by the diagnosis, particularly those who received it in their 30s, 40s or 50s. It explains difficulties that they have had all of their lives. It can be comforting to know that the basis of their problems is neurological and not any type of character flaw.

It is not necessary for a person to have a diagnosis to work with me. When an individual is concerned about the accuracy of his diagnosis, I explain that in coaching we focus on developing skills and taking action to reach goals. There is no need for any diagnostic label. So far, this reasoning has been successful.

When discussing personal challenges I stress that every human being has limitations of one kind or another. A client should not interpret this exercise to be a review of deficiencies. I state clearly that the information will be used to identify occupations that emphasize the person's strengths, and minimize their areas of weakness.

I place limitations into two categories. The first category is limitations that can be mitigated by learning new skills, utilizing assistive technology or with job accommodations. The second category is limitations that an individual cannot do much about. Knowledge of these enables a person to avoid occupations that would be frustrating or impossible to manage. For example, slow brain processing speed or poor working memory cannot be changed. Occupations that require rapid decision making or attention shifting would not be good choices for someone with these difficulties.

The *Understanding Personal Challenges* worksheet (Worksheet 5.2) is a self-assessment that I developed for my clients. It asks a person to note personal challenges that they believe could impact their success on the job.

Worksheet 5.2

UNDERSTANDING PERSONAL CHALLENGES

Read each challenge below. If you think that this challenge could impact your success once hired, check box "a." Some challenges have a second box ("b"). Check this box if your challenge is so significant that you must avoid certain jobs or work environments.

The "a" boxes you check indicate areas where you may need to learn/improve skills, or utilize assistive technology. The "b" boxes have information that will help you avoid jobs or careers that would be frustrating or impossible for you to manage. (In some cases, accommodations may mitigate a challenge.)

Challenge Areas

1. Hard to make adequate eye contact

    a. ☐ Could impact employment

2. Blurt out my thoughts (unintentionally offend/anger others)

    a. ☐ Could impact employment

3. Interrupt others

    a. ☐ Could impact employment

4. Uncomfortable meeting new people (knowing what to say/how to act)

    a. ☐ Could impact employment

    b. ☐ I must avoid jobs that require working with the public

5. Difficulty speaking clearly (tend to talk too loudly/softly/rapidly/monotone)

    a. ☐ Could impact employment

    b. ☐ I must avoid jobs that require public speaking (e.g. announcer, teacher, salesperson)

6. Difficulty following group conversations

   a. ☐ Could impact employment

   b. ☐ I must avoid jobs that require frequent group interaction

7. Take words literally and misunderstand instructions/expectations

   a. ☐ Could impact employment

8. Slow processing of verbal information

   a. ☐ Could impact employment

   b. ☐ I must avoid jobs that require talking to people and acting quickly on the information (e.g. customer service representative, emergency medical technician)

9. Easily distracted

   a. ☐ Could impact employment

   b. ☐ I must avoid work environments with noises, smells, other stimuli that will disrupt my focus

10. Not sure of how to start projects/what the steps are

    a. ☐ Could impact employment

11. Black and white thinking (hard to see options)

    a. ☐ Could impact employment

    b. ☐ I must avoid jobs that require flexibility and judgment

12. Work too slowly

    a. ☐ Could impact employment

    b. ☐ I must avoid jobs that require speed/large volume of output/ involve tight deadlines

13. Difficulty prioritizing

    a. ☐ Could impact employment

14. Hard to multitask (rapidly shift attention from one thing to another)

    a. ☐ Could impact employment

    b. ☐ I must avoid jobs with frequent interruptions, or that demand moving from one task to another quickly

15. Hard to refocus if interrupted during a task

    a. ☐ Could impact employment

16. Act impulsively, based on too little information

    a. ☐ Could impact employment

17. Problems managing time (scheduling tasks; knowing how long tasks should/will take; being on time; meeting deadlines)

    a. ☐ Could impact employment

    b. ☐ I must avoid jobs with tight deadlines, or that require the scheduling and tracking of tasks (e.g. administrative assistant)

18. Difficulty controlling emotions, especially frustration and anger (yell, shut down, walk away)

    a. ☐ Could impact employment

    b. ☐ I must avoid jobs that are stressful

19. High levels of anxiety

    a. ☐ Could impact employment

20. Problems with dual-track processing (e.g. writing while listening; looking at someone and listening)

    a. ☐ Could impact employment

    b. ☐ I must avoid jobs that require this type of information processing (e.g. customer service representative who must listen to customers and type information into a database)

21. Takes a very long time to learn new, multi-step processes, even when I take notes

    a. ☐ Could impact employment

    b. ☐ I must avoid jobs that have many administrative functions

22. Sensory processing/integration problems make me too sensitive, or not sensitive enough, to sights, sounds, smells, tastes or tactile sensations, and/or impact my balance or coordination

    a. ☐ Could impact employment

    b. ☐ I must avoid jobs or work environments that:

    _____

23. Other:

    _____

    _____

    _____

Questions

1. Which challenge areas are you willing/able to change?

2. Summarize the type of tasks and/or work environment that would be very difficult for you (example: *I would have difficulty being productive in a noisy facility where there are strong odors, such as a printing plant. Jobs where there are many deadlines, and pressure to produce quickly, would be too stressful for me*).

I also utilize the Barkley Deficits in Executive Functioning Scale (BDEFS) when individuals are concerned about organization and time management. It was developed by Russell Barkley, PhD, a specialist in ADHD and related conditions. It includes both Self- and Other-Report scales. The latter is helpful when there is disagreement between the individual and a parent, spouse or employer about performance.

The full scale includes 89 questions that are divided into five sections.

Self-organization/problem solving: items related to ease of learning new or complex activities, being able to "think on one's feet," ability to explain events in the proper sequence, and speed and fluency in problem solving.

Self-management to time: items related to procrastination, planning, motivation and poor use of time.

Self-restraint (inhibition): items related to impulsive actions and decisions, acting before considering consequences, and stopping activities and behaviors once started.

Self-regulation of emotion: items related to losing and regaining emotional control, and assessing upsetting situations more objectively.

Self-motivation: items related to the quality and quantity of work; willpower, effort and determination; delaying gratification; and achieving long-term goals (Barkley 2011, pp.40–46).

The BDEFS asks an individual to rate how often he experiences specific problems related to daily functioning, such as failing to meet deadlines, low motivation, poor memory, impulsiveness, etc.

CLIENT PORTRAIT: JOSH, PUTTING IT ALL TOGETHER

This client portrait is an example of how the four vocational "puzzle pieces"—interests, talents and skills, right work environment and the personal impact of Asperger's Syndrome—fit together to help individuals make better occupational choices.

Josh was diagnosed with Asperger's Syndrome in his early teens. He did well in school and had two friends. The transition to college was stressful. Josh had difficulty managing his schedule, and often didn't leave enough time for his projects. His parents arranged for outside assistance during his freshman and sophomore years.

For several summers during high school and college, Josh had work at landscaping companies. He enjoyed doing physical work, being outdoors and performing a variety of tasks: mowing, installing fencing and operating machinery.

Josh began coaching at age 26, eight months after earning a bachelor's degree in sociology.

On the initial coaching questionnaire, he identified his interests as: non-profits, research, model railroading, landscaping and logistics. Occupations of interest were: personal companion, survey taker, chauffeur and warehousing (he explained that he enjoys stacking items).

We spent most of the first session reviewing Josh's history. He was drawn to sociology because he was interested in human relationships and societies, particularly history and psychology. Josh wanted a job where he could help people. One possibility was at a non-profit job serving the elderly.

"How do you see yourself assisting them?" I asked.

"I could make sure that impoverished old people get their welfare checks," he said.

Josh had also thought about community organizing, and distributing literature for a non-profit at events. Since he also enjoyed research, he was curious about opportunities to conduct interviews or surveys or to analyze statistical data related to public policy initiatives.

Josh's first coaching assignments were to:

- complete three worksheets: *Important Job Criteria and Ideal Work Environment*; *Understanding Personal Challenges*; and *Talents and Skills*

- take the SDS online.

Josh identified the following characteristics as being most important in his ideal work environment:

- low stress: no quick decisions or unexpected assignments; not too many office rules

- lots of structure: knowing *exactly* what he needs to do

- close supervision

- slow and steady work pace

- minimal interaction with others

- working outdoors: likes moving around; does not want to sit at a computer all day

- salary that will enable him to live on his own.

He identified the following personal challenges as potentially impacting employment:

- being punctual

- getting tasks done quickly

- knowing how to get started on tasks

- avoiding distractions

- allowing enough time to complete tasks

- social interaction: knowing what to say next; putting his thoughts into words; understanding other people and their problems.

On the SDS, Josh scored highest in Realistic, followed closely by Conventional. His third highest score was tied between Social and Artistic. Next was Enterprising and the lowest was Investigative.

I explained the characteristics of each Holland type to Josh. He said that the Conventional type sounded very much like him, and the Realistic type made sense, too. Since he had a strong desire to help people, he decided to focus on occupations in the RCS groups.

After reviewing the suggested occupations and his own ideas, Josh decided to explore:

- truck driver

- piano tuner

- bicycle repairer

- credit analyst

- landscape specialist

- file clerk

- police officer

- recreation aide.

He also added personal assistant and non-profit work.

Truck driver was appealing because Josh liked to drive. He could see himself as a personal assistant who drove an elderly person to doctor's appointments. Piano tuner and bicycle repair were connected to his enjoyment of music and cycling.

Josh thought that credit analysis would be interesting because he could analyze statistics and credit ratings. However, he was concerned that he would have trouble understanding what the numbers meant. Math was not his strongest subject.

File clerk was a possibility because it seemed like an easy job.

Police officers help people, as do recreation aides. Josh mused about being a camp counselor since he enjoyed children and being outdoors.

Rather than judge any of the possibilities, I wanted Josh to perform some preliminary research to learn more about each occupation. The data would help him determine the viability of each option.

So that he wouldn't become overwhelmed, I asked Josh which occupations he wanted to research first. He thought that four would be a manageable number and chose: piano tuner, credit analyst, landscaper and recreation aide.

I directed Josh to the *Occupational Outlook Handbook* (www.bls.gov/ooh) from the US Department of Labor Statistics. This is a database that describes various jobs and careers. It is available on the Internet at no charge. I gave Josh a demonstration of how to search different jobs and explained the relevance of the information.

Over the next few weeks, Josh began narrowing down his list. Some jobs were eliminated because they did not pay enough, or were seasonal or part-time. Others, such as police officer, required additional training and Josh wanted to find a job quickly. The non-profit sector held promise, especially talking to people about programs, distributing literature and entering information into a database.

At one point, Josh expressed a worry that is common among my clients. The jobs that he was exploring did not utilize his degree. He did not want to "waste" his education. I assured him that much of what he learned in college would benefit him at any job.

Interestingly, the occupation that continued to top the list was landscaping. Josh had experience of doing this type of work and enjoyed it. He was clear about his distaste for sitting behind a desk all day. "I like to move around, be outside," he said. The tasks were very structured and routine. The pace suited

Josh. While there would be some interaction with his boss and other workers, he would be by himself for most of the day. Josh said that too much people interaction made him nervous and stressed.

Ultimately, Josh contacted a landscaping company he had worked for previously. He was hired on a part-time basis with the potential for full-time hours in a few months.

OCCUPATIONAL RESEARCH

I prefer to use the *Occupational Outlook Handbook* when clients are conducting preliminary career research. It provides enough, but not too much information. Additionally, each occupational description is clearly organized into seven sections: What They Do, Work Environment, How to Become One, Pay, Job Outlook, Similar Occupations and Contacts for More Information.

The *Job Research Template* (Worksheet 5.3) allows an individual to record his impressions as he reads through a description. I emphasize that the purpose is to record *his* thoughts, concerns and questions, not to cut and paste information from the *Handbook*.

The Similar Occupations section is particularly useful because it presents other options. Sometimes a client discovers that a job he is interested in is a poor match. He might find a related occupation that is more promising.

A good example is video gaming. When I mention this at a workshop, most of the parents who are present roll their eyes and emit a knowing chuckle. There are many young people who become obsessed with playing video games, sometimes to the point where it consumes nearly all their waking hours. However, this interest can be the starting point for occupational research. There are many different jobs in the video gaming industry: game designer, programmer, animator, audio engineer, writer, tester, technical support specialist, public relations manager, as well as positions in marketing and sales. Many of these jobs require skills that are transferrable to other industries.

Usually, I demonstrate how to use the *Handbook*. It is not intuitive for most individuals. I ask the client to choose a job for the demonstration and then we go through the description section by section. I explicitly describe why the information is important ("This section describes the educational requirements. You will find out whether you need additional schooling and if so, what type"). Some clients need more than one demonstration to feel comfortable using this database.

It is also necessary for me to tell clients to email their completed job research templates to me in advance of our next coaching session. This gives me a chance to review their comments, and to read the occupational descriptions. These clients may misinterpret what they read, or overlook critical points about a job. One woman wanted to be a veterinarian because she liked being around animals, not people. She missed the fact that veterinarians have a lot of interaction with pet owners and veterinary technicians.

Occupational descriptions (in the *Handbook* and elsewhere) do not spell out aspects of a job that neurotypicals consider to be obvious. A professional or parent must act as a translator. Based on what I know or suspect about a client, I will discuss unstated expectations, such as the ability to remember sequential steps, listen and write at the same time, or manage time independently.

The template asks an individual to rate his interest in a particular occupation. I reassure clients that their rating might change as they learn more about a job or career. The rating makes it easier to prioritize the various options.

Utilizing an objective information source, such as the *Occupational Outlook Handbook*, has an added benefit. Aspergians can be quite rigid and have very inaccurate ideas about what an occupation entails. If I tell a client he is being unrealistic, I am putting myself into the role of a parent or authority figure, not a coach. Like anyone else, Aspergians do not want to be told what to do. It is important that I am perceived as an ally. Using data from an impartial source is a non-threatening way to correct mistaken perceptions.

Another valuable source of preliminary career research is job postings. I ask a client to search job boards and find four or five openings in the field he is considering. Usually we establish beforehand specifically which job boards and what job titles. Clients bring copies of the posts to their coaching session so that we can review them and notice: what tasks and skills are emphasized; necessary experience; required education; and clues about the work environment.

Worksheet 5.3

JOB RESEARCH TEMPLATE

Print or copy this form for each job that you are researching. If you are filling out the form on your computer, type your answers in the gray boxes. Otherwise write your answers in the space provided (use an additional sheet if needed).

Begin by using the *Occupational Outlook Handbook* (www.bls.gov/ooh/) to gather basic information about the job or career that you are interested in. The questions below are matched to descriptions in the *Occupational Outlook Handbook*. Click on the blue, underlined headings (e.g. What They Do, Work Environment, etc.) to read the full description. As you continue your research, you can add additional information from other sources to this sheet.

Name of job/career:

_____

1. Read the description of *what they do*. What are the primary tasks? Are there categories or specialties in this line of work (lawyers, for example, may specialize in civil or criminal law, bankruptcy or property law, etc.)? What kind of equipment or technology is used? What types of companies hire in this field?

    _____

    _____

    _____

2. Read the description of *work environment*. How is the work environment described? Is overtime or weekend hours expected? How well do you think you could work in this environment?

    _____

    _____

    _____

3. Read the description of *how to become one*. Are you currently qualified to do this work? What, if any, additional training/certification/licensure do you need now? How likely is it that you can acquire further education? How do you see yourself advancing in the field?

    _____

    _____

    _____

4. Read the description of *pay*. Are the average salaries what you were expecting?

    _____

    _____

    _____

5. Read the description of *job outlook*. Has the field undergone any major changes? How competitive is it? Is it growing or declining? Are certain jobs more abundant than others? What are the entry level jobs (note this if you would be entering this field)?

    _____

    _____

    _____

6. Review *similar occupations*. Which, if any, do you want to learn more about?

    _____

    _____

    _____

7. Based on what you have read what aspects of this job are attractive to you?

    _____

    _____

    _____

8. What aspects are unattractive?

_____

_____

_____

9. What aspects of this occupation, if any, would you find to be difficult or impossible?

_____

_____

_____

10. Based on what you know now, rate your interest in this occupation:

   ☐ a. I am very interested in this occupation and definitely want to learn more.

   ☐ b. Looks interesting; I have some concerns but will continue researching.

   ☐ c. Might be a possibility, but I do not want to actively research at this time.

   ☐ d./f. Take it off the list!

11. If you rated this job/career an A or B, which resources do you want to consult next?

   ☐ Visit job board(s) and find three to five job listings to review.

   ☐ Research occupations on another Web site, such as O*Net (www.onetonline.org).

   ☐ Google search on job/career (example: "What do veterinarians do?" "Jobs in the legal field").

   ☐ Visit the Web site of professional association.

   ☐ Read a professional journal/newsletter/blog.

Applied Career Research

After completing preliminary research, a client has usually identified between one and three occupations that appear promising. However, there are limits to what can be learned just by reading. Activities such as informational interviewing, job shadowing, internship and strategic volunteering provide a deeper understanding of an occupation.

It should not be assumed that every individual will be able to conduct all of these activities. Significant preparation is often necessary.

Informational Interviewing

Speaking to people who are working in the field of interest is an excellent way to learn more about an occupation. Informational interviewing also utilizes many of the skills required for job interviews. The majority of my clients are seeking work in the competitive labor market. This is a no-risk opportunity to practice skills they will need to get hired.

Be certain that the individual understands that the purpose is to gather information, not to ask for a job! He will probably need explicit, step-by-step guidance on how to find contacts, what questions to ask and how to request and conduct a meeting. Here are some questions that my clients intended to ask at informational interviews:

> "How can I learn to make small talk?" … "How can I tell if my communication problems are because of me, or someone else?" … "I've had 20 interviews and no job offers. Do you know why that is?" … "How does LinkedIn work?" … "I'm willing to take any job. Are there openings in your company?"

It is also important to explain that an informational interview is the individual's meeting. "You can't show up and expect that the other person is going to direct what happens," I say. A client and I discuss what to wear, what questions to ask and what to bring. I remind him to bring the contact's name, job title and telephone number. One young man showed up at a company and could not remember who he had an appointment with!

Nothing should be taken for granted, which is why I usually conduct a mock informational interview. For example, an individual may need instruction on how to introduce himself:

- Stand up.

- Look at the person and smile.

- Extend your right hand, clasp their hand, squeeze and pump your hand once or twice.

- Say your greeting: "Hello, I'm John Smith, it's nice to meet you."

Ideally, a parent or professional will be able to suggest one or two contacts from their network. That way the first meetings will be less formal and more relaxed.

An individual should determine beforehand what it is that he wants to learn. Asking very basic questions is not a good use of either person's time. I stress that a person has to prepare for an informational interview the same way he will prepare for a job interview.

Worksheet 5.4 is a "cheat sheet" that I give to clients to help them prepare the right questions to ask.

If a live, face-to-face meeting is too big a step, an individual can start online. The business networking site LinkedIn features groups for virtually any occupation or industry. There is no charge to join groups. Posting a question or comment is a way to get advice and begin networking. I work out questions or comments with a client beforehand.

Job Shadowing

Observing someone performing his job is another way to enhance understanding of an occupation. Job shadowing is particularly valuable for Aspergians since they have trouble imagining what they haven't experienced. For many, "seeing gives meaning."

Job shadowing provided several of my clients with a clearer and more realistic picture of tasks and the work environment. One who was considering public relations saw that the job required more multitasking and people interaction than she anticipated. Another who was considering speech–language pathology realized that he did not want to work one-on-one with individuals.

The job shadowing experience does not have to be extensive. My clients have arranged visits as short as two hours. As with informational interviewing, a parent, professional or perhaps even a college professor may be able to arrange job shadowing via their own networking contacts.

Worksheet 5.4

CHEAT SHEET!

Good and Bad Questions to Ask on
an Informational Interview

Good Questions

An informational interview will probably last about 30 minutes. Prepare in advance six to eight questions to ask. Your questions should enhance what you have already learned during your preliminary career research. The questions below are suggestions; feel free to add your own.

What do you like best and least about your job?

How did you get into this field?

What is the typical career track?[1]

What kind of education is required?

What is a typical day like?

What is the best way to break into the field?

Are there publications or associations that you recommend?

What surprised you about this job/industry?

What does it take to be successful?

What kind of skills and experience do employers value the most?

What are the typical work hours?

What skills are most important in this work?

What is the best way to find work in this field?

What is the salary range for [entry level, mid-level, management][2] positions?

---

1   Career track refers to the typical progression of promotions and increased responsibilities as people advance in a profession.

2   Do not ask about all job levels; ask about *your* job level. Otherwise, the individual may think that you are asking about his salary.

Do you know of other people I could talk to? May I use your name?[3]

Stealth Inquiries

These questions can give you an idea of how much multitasking and interpersonal interaction a job involves, without asking directly!

Do You Work a Lot With Other People, or Mostly by Yourself?

How would an introvert like this kind of work?

How would you describe the pace of the job?

Are there a lot of interruptions?

Would this work be difficult for someone who needs quiet time to focus on tasks?

Bad Questions

Inappropriate questions to ask at an informational interview concern basic job readiness or job search skills. It is also important to avoid queries that make you seem desperate. People want to help other professionals, not people who are desperate!

Examples of inappropriate questions:

- What jobs am I qualified for?

- How can I learn to make small talk?

- How can I tell if my communication problems are because of me, or someone else?

- I've had 20 interviews and no job offers. Do you know why that is?

- How does LinkedIn work?

- I'm willing to take any job. Are there openings in your company?

- What should I say when I'm asked about my greatest weakness?

When in doubt, check it out with someone knowledgeable, who you trust!

---

3   "May I use your name?" is asking permission to tell the new contacts who referred you. Referrals from a mutual acquaintance usually respond positively to meeting requests.

Internships and Strategic Volunteering

Internships offer the chance to try out an occupation and provide job experience to include on a résumé. It may not be possible for a student with Asperger's Syndrome to manage class work and an internship at the same time. Some do not know how to find opportunities or apply. There might be resistance to the idea due to anxiety or not understanding the future value of an internship. One young man was indignant that he should be expected to work without pay!

The individual may not understand that he will interview for the internship. Those who are unprepared will not be selected for opportunities.

Strategic volunteering is another avenue. By strategic, I mean choosing a volunteer opportunity that is related to the job the person eventually wants. Non-profits are not the only organizations that accept volunteers. For-profit businesses may welcome additional help.

Individuals should be encouraged to get this type of work experience, even if they intern or volunteer after completing college or other post-secondary schooling. Young people who do not have some type of experience are at a distinct disadvantage as they try to enter the workforce.

REVIEW: KEY POINTS ABOUT FINDING THE RIGHT JOB/CAREER

- Consider the individual's interests, skills and abilities, optimal work environment and how he is impacted by Asperger's Syndrome.

- Do not confuse interest in a topic with the ability to work in a particular field. Probe interests. Are the individual's impressions of the job accurate?

- Career tools and assessments have been developed by and for neurotypicals. They do not factor in the needs and challenges of individuals on the autism spectrum. Their literalness can result in misunderstandings of questions, or confusion about how to rate items. This can skew results.

- An up-to-date neuropsychological evaluation can provide valuable information about a person's cognitive strengths and weaknesses. This can help to inform vocational decisions.

- Occupational research should focus on the primary tasks and skills needed to perform a job. Does the individual have, or can he reasonably acquire, the necessary skills? Particular attention should be paid to the amount and type of interpersonal interaction that is required. Additionally, many entry level jobs demand strong executive functioning, which could pose a problem for some individuals.

- Generally, individuals with Asperger's Syndrome perform best in environments where they can focus on one task at a time, and where there are very clear performance expectations. They favor jobs that are structured, with tasks that have clear start and end points.

- The work environment can be as important, or even more important, than tasks for employment success. Sensory processing problems can interfere with certain types of jobs or work settings. An individual may need to avoid certain occupations, or require job accommodations.

- The more that an individual understands about how Asperger's Syndrome impacts him, the easier it will be to find a manageable job. Aspergians are a truly heterogeneous population. Not everyone experiences the same symptoms or to the same degree. Even the best job research cannot guarantee success in a certain field. Sometimes, experience is the best teacher.

- An individual may have personal limitations that can be mitigated by learning new skills, utilizing assistive technology or requesting workplace accommodations. When this is not possible, extra attention must be paid to finding jobs that emphasize strengths rather than areas of challenge.

- Informational interviewing, job shadowing and volunteering can help an individual get a more accurate idea of what it is like to work at a certain job or in a particular field. Young people will probably need extensive preparation for these activities.

Chapter 6

GETTING A JOB

Finding a job is lot different today than when I began my career. There is a much greater emphasis on networking, which immediately puts most people with Asperger's Syndrome at a disadvantage. It is no longer enough to send résumés in response to job openings. Job seekers must engage in several activities that will bring them to the attention of hiring managers. The process is often intimidating and overwhelming for Aspergians.

A job search involves many executive function tasks:

- planning a job search strategy that includes several, concurrent activities
- organizing time to search for openings, find contacts, network and plan follow-up telephone calls and emails
- prioritizing and choosing the best strategies
- researching information about a hiring manager, company or industry
- developing new strategies if current activities aren't producing results
- coping with frustration and rejection
- sustaining motivation for weeks or months.

There is also a strong "social" component:

- networking to discover job leads and contacts
- selling one's abilities on résumés and cover letters
- understanding a hiring manager's perspective to prepare strong responses to interview questions
- engaging interviewers with a pleasing appearance, warm smile and confident demeanor.

When I ask clients to tell me about their current job search activities, they usually respond with one activity: sending a résumé in response to posted job openings.

Then we talk about results. Is the individual getting invited for job interviews? Does he get second interviews and job offers? When there are no interviews, it tells me that: the person needs to work on his résumé and cover letter; isn't doing enough volume of activities to find work; or is applying to jobs for which he is not qualified. If he has been on many interviews, but doesn't receive call-backs or offers, then I know he needs to improve his interviewing skills.

I give clients a list of various job search activities, and ask which they want to use:

- one-on-one networking

- online networking

- creating a LinkedIn profile

- participating in LinkedIn groups

- searching Internet job boards

- posting a résumé on Internet job boards

- registering with a staffing firm or recruiter

- contacting college alumni / career office(s)

- joining a job seeker support group

- attending a career fair

- contacting professional association(s).

I do not assume that a person understands what these activities are, or how to utilize them. I also stress to a client that he needs to choose several activities that he can follow through on consistently. For example, only a very few of my clients would consider attending a job fair.

Individuals may be sensitive about appearing unknowledgeable about a strategy. If I ask, "Do you have any questions about contacting a staffing firm?" he might say no, even if he has no idea what a staffing firm is. Instead I ask, "What do you know about staffing firms?"

I usually get a client started with activities that do not involve interaction with others, such as creating a LinkedIn profile and posting a résumé online. Then I might suggest contacting a college career office or a staffing firm. With enough preparation, high-functioning individuals can arrange one-on-one networking—arranging meetings with one person at a time, to request advice or job leads.

I do a lot of brainstorming with clients, as this teaches me a lot about what they know and how much preparation they need. One young man who wanted an editorial job planned to contact a human resources manager for an informational interview. Another thought that *hiring manager* was a job title. It bears repeating that Aspergians usually need specific instruction on how to apply job search information from books to their situation.

For example, take résumé writing. An individual may have difficulty identifying relevant information and summarizing his experience. The result can be a long, densely packed document that obscures pertinent points. One job seeker repeated, verbatim, basic facts about Web design for each of his five previous jobs. He didn't realize that employers would surmise that he utilized basic skills in each successive position.

Others are too succinct, like Peter. Although he worked at a historical association for three years, he listed his experience simply as "researcher."

"This doesn't communicate what you did at that job," I said.

"Yes, it does," he said, "I did research."

I asked Peter to list all of his duties. Then we chose the ones that were most relevant to the type of job he was seeking. His new résumé read, "Conducted primary research using journal databases, monographs, library materials and the Internet."

Sometimes individuals have work histories that are littered with short-term jobs, under-employment or large gaps in between jobs. It can be quite challenging to cover gaps and create a reasonable work history. In these cases, a person might need job training, preferably in an area where there is high job growth. State vocational rehabilitation agencies may be able to fund training, as well as provide insight into a local job market.

JOB SEARCH TIPS
Manage Unrealistic Expectations

A discrepancy analysis can be useful when a person is confused about his qualifications, the amount of money he can earn or the responsibilities that he can handle. I ask a client to print listings of four or five jobs that he is interested in or has already applied for. I create two columns on a sheet of paper. In the left column, we list aspects of the jobs that match the client's skills, experience and education. In the right column, we list discrepancies. We can then discuss where he has to make adjustments. Once again, this objective, fact-based approach lets the data do the talking.

Decode the Language of Job Posts

For individuals with Asperger's Syndrome, job posts are filled with ambiguous and confusing requirements. What does it mean to have "good" communication skills, or work well on a team, or to multitask? Unless my background and skills match *exactly*, how can I be qualified? How would I know whether I am "deadline-driven" or a "self-starter?" What is the difference between preferred and required experience?

Clients have sometimes taken the description so literally that they disqualify themselves from jobs that they can handle. A young man with 19 months of data entry experience did not believe that he was qualified for a job that asked for "2-plus years" of experience. It took a lot for me to convince him to apply. "But I don't *have* two years of experience!" he insisted.

There have been several occasions where recent college graduates believe that their education, or a high GPA, qualifies them for manager or director-level positions. Some individuals have a hard time reconciling that job titles are not the same from one organization to another. They don't see how they could be qualified as an assistant, specialist *and* clerk.

Worksheet 6.1 is a handout I give to clients to help them better understand the language of job posts.

Worksheet 6.1

DECODING THE LANGUAGE OF JOB POSTS

Correctly interpreting the language of job openings is useful during several stages of the job search:

- *Preliminary career research*: job openings define job tasks and required skills, and help you determine whether a job or industry is a good match for your interests and abilities.

- *Writing résumés and cover letters*: enables you to include information about your experience, skills and education that matches employer needs.

- *Job seeking*: saves time and effort when you apply only to jobs that you are qualified for.

- *Interview preparation*: helps you prepare responses that emphasize employer needs.

Job posts contain clues about:

- primary job tasks

- skills needed to complete tasks

- the type and amount of experience needed

    ○ industry-specific (e.g. health care, informational technology)

    ○ number of years

    ○ level (e.g. entry, senior, manager, director)

- work environment

    ○ pace, level of supervision, level of responsibility, etc.

- amount and nature of interaction with others.

When reading job postings, be aware that:

- The most important skills are listed first.

- Primary tasks are usually mentioned in the overall job description, and then repeated in lists of requirements and/or duties.

- Key skills are often emphasized with words and phrases such as: *"extensive experience..." "strong knowledge of..." "proven track record..." "expert..." "exceedingly..." "excellent..." "take charge of..." "heavy contact with..."*

- Non-negotiable items are identified with phrases like: *"extensive/ verifiable experience in..." "must include..." "do not apply unless you meet these requirements."*

- Negotiable items are identified with phrases like: *"preferred..." "desired..." "the ideal candidate will have..." "is a plus..."* and *"should be familiar with..."*

- The pace of work environment is indicated with phrases such as: *"must work well under pressure"..."deadline-driven environment"..."hectic"... "fast paced."*

- The phrase *"ability to get along with diverse groups of people"* refers to an environment where you must adapt to individuals with different needs and work styles. *"Self-starter"..."fast learner"..."independent"* mean that you are expected to initiate and complete tasks without a lot of supervision. *"Ability to maintain a sense of humor"* means, "Watch out! This is a stressful, frustrating job!"

- The ubiquitous requirements for "good people skills/teamwork" and "ability to multitask" are relative. They can mean very different things depending on a particular job, industry and company. Refer to the information you gathered during preliminary research and informational interviews, and what you already know about an industry.

How to Read Job Postings

1. Highlight or underline key words and phrases.

2. Notice which requirements are repeated in the posting.

3. Pay attention to the types of tasks and skills that are emphasized: technical, organizational, interpersonal.

Conduct Sample Searches

It should not be assumed that an individual knows how to search job boards. I determine with a client which boards he will search, what job titles he will use and the geographic region. The last point should not be overlooked. One man spent hours applying for retail sales associate positions in far-away states, believing that an employer would pay for him to relocate. A young woman didn't know to filter search results by region, and had to sift through hundreds of openings that weren't relevant.

Aaron was concerned that he might overlook the right job. Due to his weak drive for central coherence (see Chapter 1), he did not think to narrow his search by any criteria *except* geographic region. Each day he patiently read through dozens upon dozens of openings for all manner of occupations.

Once a client and I determine his search criteria, I suggest, "Let's do a sample search and make sure these are the right terms."

Control the Flow of Information

Less is more for Aspergians. Too many information sources will overwhelm an individual, as happened to Mike.

After being laid off, Mike attended a workshop on how to find a job. It was sponsored by his state unemployment office. After returning home, he called me.

"How was the seminar?" I asked.

"I'm paralyzed," he replied. "I don't even know where to begin!"

I was able to arrange a coaching session for the next day. Mike arrived carrying a notebook bulging with handouts. He flipped through a mound of paper and removed a four-page document. Arranged in two columns per page were the names and URLs of job boards, government job sites and national industry associations.

"Am I supposed to look at all of these sites every day?" Mike asked.

He was not being a wise guy, resistant or lazy. The amount of information, and pace at which it was presented, was too much for him to process. Additionally, Mike wasn't thinking in terms of the big picture. Rather than quickly scan the URLs and choose several that were most applicable, he was preparing to scrutinize each one to see whether it might be useful. Having a master's degree did not change Mike's autistic information processing style.

Unless there is a special reason not to, I suggest that clients limit the number of job boards they search to three, which is what Mike did. There are several boards that aggregate posts from other sites (including company Web sites), which saves time and simplifies the search. Such sites include www.indeed.com and www.simplyhired.com.

Plan Daily Job Search Activities

Unless activities are scheduled they probably will not get done. Some individuals need to choose specific times of day to work on their job search. I find that follow through is better when a daily or weekly schedule is printed and placed where the individual will see it each day.

Clients who don't write down assignments promptly forget what they agreed to do. I have had success using the incredibly simple *Daily Job Search To-Do List* (Worksheet 6.2). Again and again, individuals who previously had trouble keeping commitments were able to complete activities they wrote down on this form.

Break Tasks into Small, Specific Steps

"Update résumé" is an assignment for a neurotypical, not for an Aspergian. A workable plan looks like this:

1. Write an objective, which is one or two sentences describing the type of job you are seeking (see examples).

2. List each job you have had, beginning with the most recent. Start the listing with the job title and company name in bold-face font.

3. Describe the primary responsibilities, job tasks, skills used and the results that were achieved. See example and notes from the coaching session.

4. End each job listing with the length of employment. Example: March 2010–September 2014.

Worksheet 6.2

DAILY JOB SEARCH TO-DO LIST

Monday

(_____) date

- _____
- _____
- _____
- _____
- _____

Tuesday

(_____) date

- _____
- _____
- _____
- _____
- _____

Wednesday

(_____) date

- _____
- _____
- _____
- _____
- _____

Thursday

(_____) date

- _____
- _____
- _____
- _____
- _____

Friday

(_____) date

- _____
- _____
- _____
- _____
- _____

CLIENT PROFILE: THE BAKER

Susan discovered the culinary arts by accident. Initially, she wanted to work with animals. She tried dog grooming, but customers complained that she was too slow. The environment was also exhausting: too many people and noises. A front-desk position at a veterinary office lasted less than two weeks. Susan was so distracted by the animals that she had trouble focusing on the computerized appointment calendar. She was let go because there were too many scheduling conflicts. Dog walking was out of the question. "I can't stand very cold or very warm weather, or being outside when it's raining," she said.

To earn some money, Susan next took a part-time job at a local bakery. She enjoyed the work so much that she enrolled in culinary school a few months later. Now, it had been seven months since graduation and she still had not found work.

For Susan, the prospect of job hunting was completely overwhelming.

"I've read books and looked at Web sites," she said, "but I have absolutely no idea of what to do."

"How did you get your first bakery job?" I asked.

"My mother's friend owns the bakery," Susan said. "I contacted her after I graduated, but the only opening was for bread baking."

Susan was interested in baking desserts *only*, and also enjoyed decorating cakes and pastry. Her résumé needed only minor adjustments, and she had a strong portfolio to show potential employers.

I explained how to do basic networking, and we made a list of the people she already knew. After she wrote down the names of several instructors at the culinary school, I asked Susan about former classmates who might know of openings.

"I didn't have any friends at school," Susan said, without emotion.

We moved on and made a list of the type of companies she wanted to work at: bakery, supermarket, catering company, a restaurant or hotel. Next, we specified which job titles she would use to search job boards.

Together we did a test search on a job board to see what opportunities would come up.

Susan was surprised to see about a dozen listings that fit her criteria. I asked her to pick one that we could review together.

Baker & Cake Decorator, Sal's Bakery

sal's bakery a premiere bakery and catering company has an opening for a part-time cake decorator. Ideal applicants will thrive in a fast paced environment, have excellent communication skills, and be able to multi-task. We are seeking an experienced candidate who is passionate about baking and with knowledge of working with butter cream and non-fondant decorating.

I asked Susan what she thought about the opening.

"The name of the bakery isn't capitalized in the first sentence," Susan said, "but it is capitalized in the title. I wonder if it is capitalized on their sign."

"What else," I asked.

"There should be a comma in the first sentence after 'bakery,' and after 'company.' There are several grammatical errors. That is a red flag that they might produce poor products," Susan said.

"I noticed the grammatical and punctuation errors, too," I said. "But my guess, based on the name of the store and its location, is that this is a small, family-run business. The owner may be a terrific baker, but not a very good writer. I'm curious what you think about the job itself."

"Technically speaking, I can bake what they want," replied Susan, "but I don't think that I'm qualified."

"How come?" I prompted.

"It says that you need excellent communication skills, have to be a team player, and have to work in a fast-paced environment," she answered.

Susan's preoccupation with grammatical errors was distracting her from evaluating the actual job. Her concerns about the interpersonal interaction and a fast-paced environment were understandable. But I wondered just how much interaction there would be, particularly in a small shop.

I asked Susan about the process of baking and decorating.

"It sounds like you do most of the work by yourself," I observed.

Susan agreed. We made an educated guess that the communication would involve exchanging factual information about ingredients, quantities and time frames. I asked whether she had trouble meeting deadlines at her first baking job or in culinary school. She explained that when she was focused on a task, deadlines were not a problem.

"It seems to me that you can handle the pace," I said.

"Yes. But I just don't know if this is the right job," she said.

"That is something you will find out, if you get an interview," I explained. "The employer will evaluate your skills and experience. You will also have the chance to ask questions to see whether the job is the right match. You can always decline a job offer."

Susan agreed to apply to Sal's Bakery, as well as several other jobs.

We also found a specialty Web site that listed jobs in food service. Susan sent inquiries to local bakeries, contacted the culinary school's career office and reached out to several instructors.

Interviewing was not a problem for Susan. She was articulate, had a strong portfolio and demonstrated enthusiasm for the work. Employers mostly asked technical questions about baking and decorating.

Within a few weeks of our first meeting, Susan found a job with a commercial baker. I never learned whether she interviewed at Sal's, or if there are capital letters on their sign.

INTERVIEWING

For the majority of Aspergians interviewing is a complex social event fraught with unspoken expectations and confusing protocols.

Neurotypicals usually prepare for interviews by practicing how to answer anticipated questions, researching an organization and learning about the people they will meet. Aspergians do these things, too. However, there are additional details to work out. Here are examples of questions and concerns from some of my clients:

- Why do I have to introduce myself to the interviewer, when I already have an appointment?

- How can I remember to simultaneously make eye contact, smile and shake hands?

- What do I say after I introduce myself?

- How do I know where to sit (if the interviewer doesn't tell me)?

- Why was I asked about previous jobs that were already listed on my résumé?

- Why should I say that I want the job, when I want to go home and think about it?

- How closely should I follow the interviewer when we're walking to his or her office?

- What if I remember a question when I'm at the elevator?

Every one of these queries was from a person with at least an associate's degree. Several came from individuals with advanced degrees who were in their mid-30s and early 40s. The reason I mention this is because career counselors, vocational rehabilitation specialists and employers have told me that they find it difficult to understand Asperger's Syndrome. Specifically, they wonder how individuals who are bright and college educated could ask such questions. To me, the questions illustrate quite eloquently what it really means to have impaired social understanding. It has nothing to do with intelligence or education. It is a difference in the way a person's brain processes information.

Diane began working with me after two years of searching for a job that would utilize her master's degree. She guessed that she had been on 15 to 20 interviews during this time. She was only invited for a second interview on one occasion. Looking directly at me she said with great sincerity, "I want you to teach me how to lie on interviews, so I can get hired."

"What do you mean?" I asked.

"You know," she said, "lie, like neurotypicals do."

After more probing, I learned that Diane believed that most advice about interviewing encouraged people to be dishonest. I asked for an example.

"A friend said that when I'm asked about my weaknesses, I can't be honest and say making small talk and being around strangers," she answered. "So I have to lie and say something else."

Concern about lying on interviews is a a recurring theme in my practice. Jack was fresh out of college and seeking his first job as a writer.

He had no trouble articulating his passion for writing, and interest in psychology and politics. He could talk about a successful internship at a local newspaper. However, some of Jack's responses were *too* honest. He bristled at my suggestion that he not bring up his tendency to procrastinate and miss deadlines. He saw nothing wrong with describing himself as "ornery" when co-workers didn't like his ideas.

By the end of the coaching session, Jack's ire was palpable.

"You want me to lie at interviews," he said.

"No, what I'm asking you to do is *edit* what you say, based on the context of the situation," I explained. "If you tell a potential employer that you have trouble meeting deadlines and getting along with other people, they won't want to hire you."

As I slowly and carefully described the difference between lying and editing, Jack's demeanor changed. He apologized for his anger.

"I didn't mean to be so defensive," he said, "but I get so annoyed! How come I have an IQ of 140, but don't get the simple stuff?"

Preparing for interviews can be a very frustrating experience for Aspergians. I have frequently been asked, "Why can't I just tell an employer what I can do?"

Literal mindedness and an absence of guile can result in unusual responses to interview questions, as in these client examples:

Interviewer: "Why should I hire you over the other candidates?"

Job seeker: "I don't know how to answer that, because I haven't met the other candidates."

Interviewer: "What is your greatest weakness?"

Job seeker 1: "I don't know how to make small talk."

Job seeker 2: "My self confidence is very low."

Job seeker 3: "I'm not a morning person."

Interviewer: "Why do you want to work here?"

Job seeker: "I need a pay check."

Interviewer: "Where do you see yourself in five years?"

Job seeker: "In Boston."

Interviewer: "What questions do you have for me?"

Job Seeker: "Does the company pay overtime?"

An individual also may not be aware of nonverbal messages he is sending by not smiling, not making eye contact, or arriving inappropriately dressed or groomed. The stress of traveling to a new place and interacting with strangers can provoke anxiety that will be apparent at an interview.

Dean was a drafter who had been laid off from his only job after college. He had secured the position following an internship at the company. Now, nearly nine months after the layoff, he was still unemployed. He was personable, made a nice appearance and had been on a number of interviews. For some reason, there were no offers.

We began with a list of questions he remembered being asked, as well as some that might come up. We brainstormed responses and Dean made notes of the key points.

Re-energized, Dean began networking. He emailed two former professors, a former college classmate, his former supervisor and a co-worker. He forwarded a copy of his résumé and asked about job leads.

Dean's father helped him practice his responses to the interview questions. We began role playing interviews. As Dean's skill and confidence increased, I changed the wording of questions, and asked new ones that we hadn't specifically practiced. Dean picked up on what I was doing right away.

After three months of coaching, Dean had made great improvements in his interviewing skills. However, he still had difficulty summarizing his role at his previous job. He would forget key tasks, explain events in the wrong order and get sidetracked on irrelevant tangents. No matter how hard he practiced, he could not clearly explain his abilities.

There's got to be another way, I thought. He couldn't create a portfolio of work samples. But it was clear that he needed cues in order to explain his expertise. Then it hit me: perhaps he could use infographics (visual representations of information) to create "project reviews" to show prospective employers. The idea was to create a one-page summary of a relevant project that was illustrated with a few charts, graphs and call boxes. Dean would hand one to the hiring manager, and keep a copy for himself. He could then talk through the project and fill in details.

Dean was enthusiastic about the idea. We chose three projects that best represented his skills, and outlined what information should be included on each project review.

After presenting the project reviews at several interviews, two companies invited Dean back for a second round of interviews.

This story is a reminder about having realistic expectations of an individual. When several months of diligent practice didn't produce the result Dean needed, it was time to try something else.

The challenges of some Aspergians are very noticeable or hard to control. Someone who has great difficulty making adequate eye contact, organizing his thoughts or speaking clearly when he is practicing with *you* will not magically transform into a savvy interviewer outside of your office. For some individuals, it makes sense to disclose their Asperger's Syndrome during an interview.

If an individual decides to disclose, work with him on what to say. One of my clients planned to quote technical jargon from the DSM. Another launched into a long story about Temple Grandin and historical figures believed to be on the autism spectrum. A disclosure statement should briefly explain unusual behavior and emphasize positives: "Because of my Asperger's Syndrome, I may not look enthusiastic, but my data entry skills are excellent and I'm excited about this position." (Disclosure and accommodations are discussed in Chapter 8.)

TIPS FOR INTERVIEW PREPARATION
Explain the Employer's Perspective
An individual may not fully understand how he is being evaluated. Some believe that a high IQ or GPA alone will lead to job offers. I explain that employers look at whether a person has the right skills and experience, is reliable and can get the job done, and can work well within a group. The last point is important to emphasize because every job involves at least *some* interaction with others.

Aspergians may resist actions that they consider silly or unimportant, such as feigning great interest in a job or company. To illustrate the importance of enthusiasm, I sometimes pretend to be a job candidate and give an exaggerated example of a bored response. I ask the client whether he would want to hire such a candidate. Most get my point.

Denham Resources is a California-based recruiting, staffing and human resources consulting firm. It produces videos on how to answer interview questions. Skits feature "good," "bad," and "ugly" responses. The latter are quite exaggerated and clearly illustrate poor verbal and nonverbal communication. The videos can be found by searching Denham Resources Interview Videos on YouTube.

Some individuals become upset at what they perceive as the unfairness or superficiality of the interviewing process. Rather than argue as to the validity of their feelings, I use logic: "I see your point, however, you are competing in the neurotypical job market. You need to show how your abilities match what employers want, or they will choose someone else."

Brainstorm Answers to Anticipated Questions

I am very interested to hear how an individual has answered, or plans to answer, interview questions. This tells me how much he understands about interviewing. I evaluate whether an individual:

- takes questions literally and doesn't understand what the interviewer wants to know

- provides too much detail and needs help prioritizing and summarizing relevant points

- offers responses which are too short because he doesn't know how to describe his skills

- speaks in a manner that is hard to understand or suggests boredom or poor preparation.

Brainstorming also allows me to draw out his abilities and experience. I always build off of what a client tells me about his skills, so that he will feel confident about his responses. If he offers an answer that is inappropriate, I "translate" what a potential employer would hear.

When Samuel was asked to describe a personal failure, he mentioned his inability to interview well!

"To a hiring manager that sounds like you don't want to put in the effort to prepare for interviews," I said. "I know that's not the case, and now you are working hard to learn those skills." I explained that the purpose of the question was to see whether a person took responsibility for mistakes and could learn from them. Based on that understanding, Samuel found an example from his senior year of college that demonstrated perseverance.

Create a Plan for Interview Practice

Aspergians often don't realize that they need to practice before an interview. It is common for clients to tell me that their preparation is to scan a list of possible questions, and think about what they will say. They are surprised when I explain that they need to practice their responses out loud, and do this many times.

A customizable template like *How to Prepare Answers to Interview Questions* (Worksheet 6.3) can help individuals organize and practice responses. It offers guidelines for how long answers should be (usually three to five sentences). The use of bulleted phrases is deliberate. It reminds a person of the points he wants to make, and prevents him from memorizing answers word for word. Additionally, I tell clients to use a conversational tone when they practice.

I encourage clients to make audio or video recordings of their practice sessions, so that they have an idea of how they sound and/or appear to an interviewer. We might also arrange a recording of a mock interview session.

Regular practice sessions should be part of the individual's job search plan. Simulations, such as those offered by Perfect Interview (www.perfectinterview.com), give individuals experience answering questions in real time. Perfect Interview enables practice sessions to be recorded and forwarded to others for feedback.

If I have any doubt about a client's personal presentation, I ask him to come to a role play dressed as if it were a real interview. This includes bringing whatever items he normally would.

DUAL LANDMINES: PRE-EMPLOYMENT PERSONALITY TESTING AND BEHAVIORAL INTERVIEW QUESTIONS

Pre-employment personality tests and behavioral interview questions present real hurdles for job seekers with Asperger's Syndrome.

Many organizations use pre-employment testing to screen job applicants. The tests measure technical skills, aptitudes and intelligence, as well as personality traits and emotional intelligence.

There is debate about whether personality testing discriminates against individuals with certain developmental, cognitive and communication disorders. In the United States, pre-employment testing is legal as long as it does not violate the Americans with Disabilities Act (ADA). The ADA prohibits employers from using testing to screen out individuals with disabilities, unless such screening is consistent with business necessity. For example, if a job requires the ability to lift heavy boxes, candidates may be screened for disabilities that impact their strength or mobility.

It can be argued that personality testing puts individuals on the autism spectrum at a disadvantage. To understand a question and choose the appropriate response, a person must be able to infer the motives and intentions of others, understand situational context, and imagine abstract scenarios. It is my experience that Aspergians are completely confused by such tests.

Here is a sample question that was sent to me by a reader of my newsletter, the *Asperger's & NLD Career Letter*:

Jill placed candy bars for sale for her youth organization in the break room. Jack took a candy bar during his break and then returned to work without paying for it. What is the logical reason for his behavior?

1. Jack was late from his break and forgot to pay.

2. Jack knows Jill and thinks it is okay.

3. Jack thinks he deserves a free snack.

4. Jack believes any snack left out should be free.

The reader asked, "What is logical about any of these options? How, without further insight into Jack, can one presume to know his reasoning?"

This is an impossible question to answer when the respondent believes that it is about a specific individual named Jack. How could one know what Jack was thinking without any information about him? However, a neurotypical intuitively understands that the question is not about Jack. It is about the *test taker*. The response that is chosen reflects his attitudes, personality traits and beliefs, as well as how he interacts with others. There is also a tacit understanding that one must try to select a response that reflects characteristics the employer is seeking.

We can presume that Jill put a sign near the candy, stating the cost, and that proceeds would benefit a charity. Response 3 suggests that Jack is dishonest, selfish and inconsiderate of his co-worker. From a psychological perspective, this answer could be seen as reflecting characteristics of the test-taker, and/or how he views and treats other people. Responses 2 and 4 suggest similar negative characteristics.

Choosing response 1 suggests an entirely different perspective. The presumption is that Jack was distracted and simply forgot to pay for the candy; an innocent mistake. Selecting this answer could reflect a test taker who is trusting of others, tolerant of mistakes, and understanding.

The use of personality testing was successfully challenged in a 2005 court case. In *Karraker v. Rent-A-Center* a court ruled that use of the Minnesota Multiphasic Personality Inventory (MMPI) in pre-employment screening violates the ADA. The court found that the MMPI constituted a medical examination, which violates the ADA when administered prior to a job offer. It was also decided that its purpose was to screen out applicants with mental illnesses (Equip for Equality 2005).

At the time of this writing, nearly ten years after that decision, personality tests remain popular. Many job seekers are required to takes these tests, even when submitting online applications. Although a candidate can request an exemption as an accommodation, an employer is under no obligation to comply. According to the Job Accommodation Network:

> If the test is a requirement of the application process, the job, class or program, or licensing credentials, the test-taker with a disability will probably have to take the test. The test-taker with a disability may, however, ask for an accommodation to assist with the taking the test. (Job Accommodation Network 2010, p.6)

It is unlikely that an employer would consider explaining the context of questions and the intentions of others to be reasonable accommodations. There are companies that offer practice screening tests for job seekers. SHL Group (www.shldirect.com), for example, offers advice and tips for test taking, and practice tests that can be accessed at no charge.

Behavioral interviewing is based on the premise that past performance is a good predictor of future behavior. It is a popular method for teasing out how a person performs under pressure, how well he can work on a team, and his leadership and problem solving abilities. "Tell me about a time when you dealt with a difficult customer" is an example.

The problem for Aspergians is that behavioral interview questions are often about abstract topics, and focus on aspects of interpersonal communication. Imagine trying to answer a query about working on a team, when you are not sure what teamwork means! When Dan was asked for an example of making a mistake, he recounted an incident where he angered his boss by asking the same question several times, due to anxiety. Another client, Laurie, mentioned being fired because she worked too slowly.

I am usually able to guess the types of behavioral questions that will be asked, based on the job. Candidates for customer service-oriented positions will undoubtedly be asked about dealing with an angry or unreasonable customer. One can reasonably assume that there will be questions about working with others and handling conflict.

I have had success using the SAR method to prepare very high-functioning clients for behavioral interviews. It is an acronym that stands for Situation, Action, Results. The job seeker describes a situation he faced, the action he took and the outcome that was achieved.

Initially, it can seem overwhelming to prepare to answer these questions. However, as I point out to clients, a single SAR story can usually answer several different questions. A story about making a mistake could apply to working under pressure, dealing with a situation that didn't go as planned and problem solving. Four or five SAR stories can satisfy a broad range of inquiries (although one story cannot be used over and over during an interview).

It is wise to anticipate some resistance to interview preparation. I remember a discussion with a man who refused to answer questions about weakness.

"I don't think in terms of failure, only learning," he said.

"That is an excellent way to frame your response to that question," I said. "Simply refusing to answer it makes you seem hard to get along with, or arrogant."

This man had been on 15 interviews with no success. He had advanced education and skills that were in high demand. He saw that many of his college classmates had already found jobs. It took 15 unsuccessful interviews before he was willing to change how he responded to questions. Two weeks after doing this, he accepted a job offer.

Worksheet 6.3

HOW TO PREPARE ANSWERS TO INTERVIEW QUESTIONS

Use this worksheet to plan your responses to these common interview questions. The use of bullet points allows you to practice your responses in a conversational tone. Memorizing answers word for word will make you sound mechanical and over-rehearsed.

Process

1. Review your preliminary career research, notes from informational interviews and proving of skills for writing your résumé. What are the top requirements for this occupation? How do you meet them?

2. Review the job post. What are the three to five most important criteria the employer is looking for? How do you meet them? Why are you interested in working for *this* company?

3. Choose one or two resources (books or Web sites) and research typical questions and suggested responses. So that you don't become overwhelmed, work on two or three questions at a time.

4. Be sure that you understand what is really being asked (don't take the questions too literally).

5. Ask someone you trust to review your responses and make suggestions.

Generally, your answers should be between three to five sentences long. Too little information doesn't convey your skills and abilities. Too much information will confuse the person who is interviewing you. *If the interviewer wants more information, he or she will ask.*

Key Concept: Understanding the skills needed for the job, and proving your qualifications, makes it easier to answer interview questions. Prepare examples that show how you applied key skills and the results you achieved. One way to do this is the SAR method: **S**ituation...**A**ction...**R**esults (describe a situation, the action you took and the results achieved).

Plan Your Responses to Anticipated Interview Questions

1. Tell me about yourself.

   Since this is a summary of your background, and why you want the specific job, your response can be longer and include four or five key points.

   Key points:

   - _____
   - _____
   - _____
   - _____
   - _____

2. Why did you choose this field?

   Key points:

   - _____
   - _____
   - _____

3. What are your greatest strengths?

   Key points:

   - _____
   - _____
   - _____

4. What are your greatest weaknesses?

   Key points:

   - _____
   - _____
   - _____

5. Describe your best and worst boss.

Key points BEST:

- _____

- _____

- _____

Key points WORST:

- _____

- _____

- _____

(Author's Note: Questions can be customized based on the type of job an individual is seeking.)

Chapter 7

KEEPING A JOB

As difficult as it is to get hired, for many Aspergians the real challenge is keeping a job. For some the difficulty is interpersonal communication and for others it is executive function. Or, it is a combination of both. Co-morbid conditions, such as depression and anxiety, can also undermine a person's ability to meet performance expectations.

Even when a person is able to maintain steady employment, he may need to expend considerable energy—and endure extreme stress—to do so.

The most common job-related problems for my clients are:

- alienating co-workers with intrusive or odd behavior, or inappropriate remarks

- problems understanding an employer's expectations

- conflicts with a supervisor/co-worker(s)

- not following directions or asking for help

- inability to learn and/or perform tasks quickly enough

- poor problem solving skills.

Communication problems often appear to be attitude or behavior problems. Misunderstandings can quickly become disciplinary actions, particularly when a person is considered "hard to work with." Aspergians can be slow to recognize that there is a problem or to take action to solve it. It is not uncommon for individuals to lose their jobs without knowing why.

The following story illustrates how complicated work becomes for someone who does not intuitively understand the "rules" of interpersonal interaction.

CLIENT PORTRAIT: DANIEL IS DRIVING US NUTS!

As Daniel recalled, his love of computers began in sixth grade. By high school, he knew that he wanted to work in high tech and one day become a programmer. After earning his degree in computer science, he had little trouble finding his first job.

When we met, Daniel was 29 years old. He had lost two jobs and had now just been placed on probation by his supervisor. He had been at this latest programming job for six months. His boss, Ryan, placed Daniel on probation because of the numerous complaints about Daniel's behavior. When various incidents were brought to Daniel's attention, his behavior would improve for a week or two. Then his disruptive conduct would resume. His supervisor was losing patience, particularly after a co-worker reported an incident where she felt threatened.

Daniel's employer knew that he had Asperger's Syndrome. Ryan admitted that he was frustrated because he didn't know how to help Daniel. He agreed to speak with me about Daniel's performance, and what he needed to change to keep his job.

"Overall, the quality of Daniel's work is good," said Ryan. "His behavior is the problem. I've told him repeatedly that he needs to develop a more professional demeanor. The message doesn't seem to get through."

Ryan wanted Daniel to accept responsibility for errors. "He always wants to be right," Ryan said, "or he tries to hide his mistakes." He said that Daniel also needed to listen better, and work more slowly to avoid careless errors. He was puzzled by Daniel's sense of priorities.

"He will spend half an hour trying to fix a minor glitch, and then forget to address a major bug," he said.

Daniel asked the same question again and again. "Usually, he asks about a procedure that he has been doing for months. I've told him to make notes that he can refer to, but for some reason he doesn't do it," explained Ryan.

The bigger problem concerned Daniel's interactions with co-workers. "He's driving people crazy," said Ryan.

When Daniel became agitated about a problem at work or in his personal life, he would "make the rounds" to several of his co-workers. One by one, he would interrupt their work and share his story. At first, they listened patiently and tried to help. However, they soon tired of the frequent interruptions and became irritated that Daniel didn't act on their advice. Several complained that the topic of conversation was always Daniel. He never inquired about anyone else.

A recent incident involved Daniel's habit of eavesdropping and then joining conversations. Noticing two of his colleagues conversing in the break room he walked up and said, "It looks like you are having a private conversation. Can I join you?"

One woman replied with a curt, "No!"

Daniel then began apologizing, over and over. The woman became irritated and left the break area. Anxious and angry, Daniel followed her, apologizing and asking whether she was upset. When she arrived at her cubicle, Daniel blocked the entrance, at which point she ordered him to leave. She filed a harassment complaint with the human resources department.

"What's going right?" I asked Ryan, holding my breath.

"A lot," Ryan said. "Daniel works hard and gets the job done. He is a pleasant person. We want him to succeed, but we can't ignore the behavioral issues. I'm not looking for miracles, just sustained improvement."

At the end of our discussion, I had the following list of what Daniel needed to change:

- Work more slowly, check work, admit mistakes.

- Write down questions about an assignment and ask them all at once.

- Make notes to refer to rather than keep repeating the same questions.

- Act professionally in the office; stop over-reacting and muttering when upset.

- Listen and follow instructions.

- Stop interrupting co-workers to ask advice.

Daniel and I reviewed the list. He was amenable to all points and said that he was highly motivated to "become less annoying."

My strategy was to address the most disruptive behaviors first. One of these was Daniel's habit of calling co-workers, three and four times per hour, to ask when they would finish a task so that Daniel could begin his part of the process. David saw this as a way to plan his workday.

"People are annoyed when you keep calling to ask when they'll finish their work," I said. "How else can you find out when you'll be able to start your part of the procedure?"

"I could send them emails," Daniel said. "Multiple emails would be less annoying than phone calls, because you can delete an email."

"Emails are not as intrusive," I agreed, "but what message do you think it sends to your co-workers when you ask them every 10 or 15 minutes when they will be done?"

Daniel thought for a while.

"That I don't trust them to get their work done," he said.

"Yes," I replied, "they also might think that you don't listen to them, or that you are acting like their supervisor."

"Or, that I am invading their space," Daniel said. "Last Friday, when the accounting manager came to my desk several times with questions, I was getting annoyed."

After brainstorming several possible solutions, we figured out that Daniel could wait until after his lunch break to contact his co-workers. On most days he received their code by noon. This gave him plenty of time in the afternoon todo his work. The new rule was that if code had not arrived by 1:30pm, he would send *one* email to inquire about timing. If there was no response by 4:30pm, he would make *one* phone call to check on the status. If the matter was still not resolved, he would talk to Ryan.

Daniel wrote this process down and agreed to post it in his cubicle.

Daniel was aware that anxiety drove much of his impulsive behavior. He had a hard time interpreting others' body language. He often couldn't tell whether others were upset with him. The uncertainty made Daniel anxious, and this triggered his compulsive interrupting and repeated questioning.

I asked Daniel to keep a log of work situations that triggered his anxiety. He did this for two weeks. We talked about how he over-reacted to imagined or minor events. We used a rating scale so that he could see the imbalance between the seriousness or urgency of a situation and his response (this technique is discussed in detail later in this chapter). We differentiated legitimate business questions from compulsive, anxiety-based queries.

Daniel also agreed to stop venting about personal problems to his co-workers. Over several weeks, we identified various strategies to help him manage his stress and anxiety at work. He committed to taking his prescribed medication regularly to improve his concentration.

After three months of coaching, I arranged another call with Daniel's supervisor. Ryan was pleased with his progress. "I don't know what you did, but *thank you*," he said.

Once the most disruptive behaviors were under control, Daniel and I began exploring what it means to "act professionally." The realization that he could control how his colleagues perceived him was a paradigm shift for Daniel. Previously, he had not made the connection that people reacted to him, negatively or positively, based on his behavior.

He began observing the behaviors of his co-workers. He noticed that they did not wheel their chairs to the entrances of their cubicles to say hello to every passerby. Or thank someone five or six times for doing them a favor. They didn't interrupt, or change the topic of a conversation to a subject they enjoyed. They didn't become over-excited and talk in loud voices or shout.

Nonverbal communication posed a challenge. Daniel said that he "forgot" to notice body language. However, it was clear that he had a very hard time *interpreting* facial expressions, gestures and tone of voice. We began with the basics, such as whether and how to enter a conversation.

Daniel's habit of eavesdropping and then interrupting with a comment or question understandably unnerved people.

"That's considered rude," I explained.

I explained the basics of entering a conversation:

- walking up to a person or group to signal one's presence

- watching for signals that one can join the discussion (e.g. person smiling, turning his body toward you, saying a greeting)

- listening to the discussion

- making comments related to the topic.

"How would you know that a co-worker was busy, and didn't want to chat with you?" I asked.

"They would tell me to go away, or tell my boss that I was bothering them," Daniel said.

"People did that when you were interrupting them too often," I said. "You're not doing that anymore. Suppose you went to your buddy Alex's cubicle to say hello. How would you know if he was too busy to talk?"

After a couple of hints, Daniel said, "He would keep looking at his computer, and he might give me very short answers."

Once Daniel mastered the basics, we began watching clips from soap operas on YouTube, with the sound turned off. Daniel could accurately guess the nature of the very dramatic interactions, but found the more subtle scenes confusing. The same was true at work.

"I went outside for a break and saw Robin and Ann talking," he said. "I walked up to them, and they ignored me. Then Robin asked, 'What is it, Daniel?' and I said, 'How's it going?' and she said, 'Fine,' and ignored me again."

It took a long and detailed analysis of the exchange before Daniel could see that his co-workers were not being rude to him. They were merely having a private conversation.

After six months of coaching, Ryan and I had another meeting. Both he and Daniel's colleagues saw a positive change. Daniel was accepting criticism, didn't interrupt co-workers to discuss personal problems and asked fewer questions. Everyone could see that Daniel was trying.

Daniel had his annual performance review after we had been working together for nine months. It was positive. He was no longer on probation status and was given a raise.

There was still plenty of material to discuss in our coaching sessions. Daniel still made mistakes, and Ryan had to give him reminders from time to time. However, Daniel was no longer considered a disruptive force in the office. Every indication was that he would continue his employment.

ADDRESSING PROBLEMS ON THE JOB

There are many reasons that an individual who is employed seeks coaching:

- poor performance review, disciplinary action, formal notice to improve

- placed on a Performance Improvement Plan (PIP)

- conflict with supervisor or co-worker

- difficulty meeting basic productivity requirements

- planning to disclose and request accommodations

- seeking a job or career that will be a better fit.

Often, I must rely on what a client tells me about his situation. Even though I know that he is telling the truth as he sees it, I remain cognizant of a reporting bias. This is not unique to people with Asperger's Syndrome. Everyone's perception is influenced by life experience, personality traits, preferences, etc. Aspergians are no different. However, their bias typically comes from confusion about interpersonal relationships and communication.

The process for assisting a client with performance problems is:

1. Gather information.

2. Identify the precipitating event.

3. Develop a plan.

4. Take action.

Step 1: Gather Information

Unless the individual is in immediate danger of being fired, our first meeting is usually focused on his background and events leading to the current situation. This information can come from several sources:

- *Individual's work history*: there are often patterns of employment difficulties, which an individual may not be aware of, or consider to be relevant. Repeated conflicts with co-workers suggest a need to improve communication skills, or find a job with less interpersonal interaction. Multiple job losses might mean that a person is in the wrong field; requires a different type of training; or needs workplace accommodations.

- *Individual's narrative about events*: the way that an individual describes his situation is revealing. What I observe in a coaching sessions is probably indicative of how the person behaves at work. Sometimes, all it takes is one question from me ("What's happening?") to trigger a 20-minute, nonstop monologue. An individual may begin talking as soon as I greet him, before he is even seated in my office. Or, he may take a few steps inside and stand awkwardly, waiting for instructions on where to sit. Clients have walked around my office, scanning the titles of books or touching decorative objects. To quell her anxiety, one woman changed chairs every 10 or 15 minutes.

Some individuals arrive loaded down with multiple tote bags. They rifle through stacks of file folders to retrieve a memo or report for me to read. Unsure of what is important, they bring *everything*.

While a client is speaking, I notice whether he looks at me, responds to my facial expressions and relates events in a sequence that makes sense. Does he drift off onto tangents? Overwhelm me with too much detail? If his theory of mind ability is weak, he might abruptly mention people I couldn't know or situations that I couldn't possibly understand. Perseverative types get stuck on a point, repeating it several times.

I gain insight into his perspective taking and problem solving abilities. Does he:

- place events within the proper context?

- magnify minor incidents?

- describe extreme emotional reactions (e.g. describing himself as "tortured" or "persecuted" at work)?

- understand how his behavior impacts others?

- try to address the problem in a reasonable way?

An Aspergian may have unrealistic expectations of the workplace. He might think that he should be fully interested and engaged throughout the day. Or that he should know how to solve every problem. Clients have been amazed to learn that their colleagues experience boredom, frustration, anxiety and anger from time to time, too. I explain that their co-workers feel these emotions but usually don't express them in the workplace.

Sometimes I discover that the presenting problem is not the real issue. Usually this happens when a person doesn't realize that his behavior is disruptive. One man was asked to stop bringing up a certain topic at meetings. He declared that his right to freedom of speech was being violated, and threatened to sue his employer.

- *Current neuropsychological evaluation*: as discussed in Chapter 6, an up-to-date neuropsychological evaluation can offer insight into performance problems related to communication and executive function. For example, it is helpful to know that poor working memory is affecting a person's ability to multitask. I can suggest compensatory strategies.

Remember, as with any testing, neuropsychological evaluations have their limitations. Testing is done in a quiet examination room, not a busy office. A person may have significant difficulty performing certain tasks in real time, even though testing suggests otherwise. I always believe what my clients tell me.

- *Information from a spouse, family member or professional:* since I provide coaching to adults, my contact is usually with the client only. When a family member is involved, it is often the parent of a young adult who makes the initial contact to learn about my services. There are occasions when I will ask permission to speak with a client's family member to clarify a complex or confusing situation.

  The family member may offer a very different perspective on the client's abilities and challenges, or current situation. One young man described minimal challenges at a retail job. However, his mother explained that he had great difficulty with multitasking and was let go when he could not learn to use the cash register.

  I worked with one man whose work experiences just didn't add up. My questions failed to clarify matters. He mentioned that his sister was trying to help him find a job. I asked whether the sister and I could talk to share some ideas. He agreed and I arranged a telephone call with her. As I began summarizing what I knew about the client's previous jobs, his sister broke in and said, "Those are complete fabrications!" This revelation explained much of my confusion trying to work with this man. Unfortunately, he did not want to admit the falsifications and we had to end the coaching.

  A client might ask that I speak with his psychotherapist or other professional. I will ask the same, if there is any question about his ability to participate in coaching. There are also times when I collaborate with clinicians who may not be familiar with workplace accommodations.

- *Performance review(s):* I ask a client whether he is willing to share one or two performance reviews when he is:

  ○ uncertain about why his performance is lacking, or how to correct it

  ○ unaware that a serious problem has occurred

  ○ concerned about losing his job when there is no evidence to support this.

- *360 evaluations*: clients who work in corporations may have received a 360-degree feedback (aka multi-rater) evaluation. A 360 is where an employee's peers, subordinates and supervisor rate various aspects of his performance. It is intended to provide a "rounded" appraisal of abilities and development areas from a variety of perspectives. These evaluations are usually part of an employee's career development, but are also used when there are performance problems. When companies retain me to coach an employee, I often conduct my own 360 evaluation.

  Feedback from co-workers is usually given anonymously via a survey. These evaluations reveal how an individual is perceived by his colleagues. The results can be eye-opening for those who have little self-awareness.

- *Speak with the individual's supervisor*: in an ideal world, I would have the opportunity to speak with every client's boss. Unfortunately, this does not happen often. The individual may have decided not to disclose, is worried that the situation will become worse or does not want his supervisor involved in the coaching.

  When a client does ask his supervisor to speak with me, nearly all of them agree. When they decline it is because the situation is too far gone.

  The obvious benefit to these conversations is that they leave no ambiguity about what needs to change. I also learn more about my client. There have been several occasions where the boss my client describes as an unreasonable tyrant turns out to be quite rational and accommodating. These conversations also give me the opportunity to explain any client behaviors that are puzzling, and set realistic expectations for what can be achieved in coaching.

  When an employee decides to work with a coach of his own volition, and at his own expense, it demonstrates that he is committed to change. I have yet to meet a supervisor who has not considered that a positive.

Step 2: Identify the Precipitating Event

The next step is to figure out what is causing the performance shortfall. The key question is *Why now?* The answer may be straightforward. The client cannot learn tasks or perform them quickly enough, is late for work, makes frequent errors, doesn't follow instructions and/or cannot get along with a boss or co-workers.

In other cases, the client is not able to adapt to change. I remember one six-week period where I had three new clients, who had all been with their employers for a decade or more. Suddenly they were not meeting expectations. In one instance, the company had been acquired and the individual could not manage the new systems. The other two clients were having trouble adjusting to new supervisors.

Anne's 15-year longevity was threatened when a new manager joined the company. It appeared that he wanted to upstage Anne whenever possible. One day, he contradicted her in a meeting and Anne became so angry that she lost her temper and cursed at him.

Although I cannot prove it, my suspicion is that the new manager sensed Anne's inability to promote her capabilities. My guess is that he wanted to get himself on the fast track for a promotion. Anne nearly lost her job over this incident. The company had a collegial atmosphere and cursing at others was not acceptable. One of the conditions for Anne's continued employment was that she work on communication skills with a coach.

There may be circumstances in a client's personal life that are impacting his productivity at work. For example:

- not taking prescribed medication or having difficulty adjusting to a new prescription

- losing an important individual, such as a spouse or significant other, parent or friend

- making a significant change, such as moving.

CLIENT PORTRAIT: TOO MUCH CHANGE

Bill's story illustrates the consequences of not being able to adapt to change.

Bill received a diagnosis of Asperger's Syndrome at age 43. He decided to get an evaluation after reading a magazine article and recognizing many of the symptoms in himself. He wondered if it was the source of his struggles at work.

For 16 years, Bill had worked at the same job with his employer. He edited academic articles to make the content accessible to lay people with an interest in science. Bill enjoyed the job and had no desire for a promotion. His performance reviews were satisfactory. He got along well with his boss, who he described as "laid back." Everything was fine until eight months earlier, when his boss retired and a replacement was hired from outside the company.

Bill's new supervisor, Jane, started making changes right away. Bill and his peers were now expected to do more substantial editing for tone, style, clarity, grammar and format. Previously, most of Bill's editing was for grammar and adherence to a style manual. His Asperger's Syndrome made it challenging for Bill to edit for clarity. He couldn't comprehend what would be too technical for readers. Additionally, since talking on the telephone made him very anxious, Bill wrote long, detailed emails to authors to discuss changes.

"Sometimes I think that I spend more time writing the emails than the author spent writing the article," he said.

When an author questioned his editing, Bill usually gave in. But now, Jane complained that the articles were too technical for the subscribers.

Greater efficiency was another of Jane's priorities. She had computerized editing software installed. The editors no longer proofread manuscripts by reading them aloud to each other. Bill was having trouble using the software. "It requires a reading speed that is three to four times faster than I am used to," he said, "and I can't keep up."

"Jane thrives on stress," he continued, "which destroys me. She will bombard me with one question after another, and I just shut down. Then she gets annoyed that I don't respond."

Bill often forgot verbal instructions from Jane. She complained that he asked too many questions that he should know how to answer. "She wants me to be proactive and find the answers on my own," he said.

Jane had given Bill a warning about his performance three months after becoming his boss. Bill disclosed his Asperger's Syndrome and requested the following accommodations:

- receive assignments in writing

- receive written directions for tasks

- meet twice-weekly with Jane to establish priorities

- be given additional training on using the editing software.

The company complied. But now, after eight months of working for Jane, Bill had been given 90 days to improve his performance or be fired. The warning said that Bill had not improved despite repeated requests. Bill believed that he was doing fine, except for one recent editing job that he "bollixed." He sent me the notice to improve and the warning from Jane.

"Both documents raise the same concerns," I said. "The warning states that despite the accommodations, there has not been significant change."

"I didn't think that the situation was that serious," Bill replied.

According to the warning, too much staff time was devoted to correcting errors in Bill's work. At one point, a freelance proofreader had to be hired because Bill made so many errors in a manuscript. (Bill identified this as his lone bollixed project.) Additionally, Jane wanted Bill to come to meetings prepared. She expressed frustration that he worked from agendas from weeks prior, that were no longer relevant.

Bill said that he was depressed and stressed. He was seeing a psychotherapist and a psychiatrist. He had no family in the area, and no friends. His workplace was 60 miles from his apartment.

Bill had had just one other job in his lifetime. He was very concerned about where he could find work, if he was fired. He described difficulty meeting multiple deadlines, multitasking and interacting with the authors and his boss. The one bright spot was a strong relationship with Pam, a fellow editor who had experience with substantive editing and project management.

We got to work.

"What do you think your boss means when she says that you need to be prepared for meetings?" I asked.

Bill thought for a while. "I could read the weekly agenda," he said. "Jane says that she is surprised that I don't bring a pad to take notes. But she never tells me that I'll need to take notes."

"She is expecting that you will come to meetings with a pad and pen, so that you will be prepared, *if* you need to write something down," I explained. "What if we make a rule that you will always bring a pad and pen to meetings?"

Bill agreed. Next, we tackled his error rate. Bill admitted that he needed to utilize project check lists and update his schedule on a weekly basis. Otherwise, he forgot critical tasks and lost track of deadlines. Then he would rush and make mistakes.

"What's getting in the way of using a check list and updating the schedule?" I asked.

"There's so much to do that I become overwhelmed," Bill said, "and before I know it, the morning is almost gone and all I've done is answer questions from Jane and read emails."

We established a new routine. Bill would update his project schedule every Monday morning. He pre-printed check lists and pinned them to his bulletin board so that he would remember to use them.

We also tackled Bill's reluctance to ask his co-workers for help. His department had four other editors plus three editorial assistants.

"They might be able to help you learn the editing software," I said, "and also give you some short cuts."

Bill resisted the idea of involving the other staff members. However, he was amenable to enlisting the help of Pam. She helped him improve his editing techniques and suggested short cuts to make projects easier to manage.

Bill's anxiety about speaking with authors on the telephone was still high. He developed a reusable email template that addressed the most common issues. It was not the ideal solution, but it did save some time.

Over the next few weeks, Jane noticed Bill's efforts and commented that he was making fewer errors. He read meeting agendas and arrived ready to participate in the discussions. He sounded hopeful that he could continue to improve his productivity. He and Pam began eating lunch together once or twice per week.

Step 3: Develop a Plan

Ideally, a client's action plan will address the most penalizing behaviors first. A conversation with the individual's supervisor will make these clear. Or they may be spelled out in a performance review. Without these sources, it is a judgment call. I think about the nature of the job, and what the greatest impediments would be to satisfactory performance.

Christine worked as a nurse in a busy private practice. She enjoyed interacting with patients but found the pace to be stressful. Nurses were allotted a set period of time for each patient visit. Lately, Christine had been falling behind schedule. She blamed this on geriatric patients, who had multiple health problems. Christine allowed her patients to talk for as long as they wanted. "Everyone knows that it is rude to interrupt," she said.

She was also behind on her patient notes.

Her supervisor told her that she needed to be more efficient.

Every day, Christine worried that if a single appointment ran over time she would be fired. One morning, she rushed to the waiting area and saw that her next patient was just coming into the building. Christine called out, "You're late! Come on! If we run over the time limit, I'll get into trouble!" Inside the examining room, Christine grumbled to the patient about the strict time allotment and shared her concerns about losing her job.

The patient complained and Christine was given a written warning. "They said that I was unprofessional and inappropriate," she said, "and now they're going to be watching me every second!"

It was clear that Christine's demeanor with patients was the top priority, followed by better time management. We worked on how she could interrupt patients in a polite way, so that appointments would not run over. A fellow nurse helped her write patient notes more quickly.

A client's action plan should:

- be written, and include specifically what the individual will do and when

- include step-by-step instructions for individuals who need them

- feature samples or examples of the finished product, when applicable

- contain contingency plans if necessary

- be placed in a location where it will be seen on a daily basis.

It should be explicitly explained that an employer expects fast and sustained improvement. When I believe that a client is in danger of losing his job, I say so.

Ron had a long history of job losses and now, once again, a conflict with a supervisor was threatening his livelihood. The situation had become so tense that exchanges between the two were monitored by a human resources representative. The stress was hard for Ron to handle. He admitted that he had over-reacted to feedback. In his anger, Ron called his boss pig-headed, emphasizing his comment by pointing his finger at him.

While we were discussing how to repair the relationship and prevent similar incidents in the future, Ron said, "I apologized for my actions. Why can't my boss just forget it?"

"You have developed a reputation for being explosive and insubordinate," I said. "There have been other occasions where you didn't react professionally when he corrected your work. My guess is that if something like this happens again you will be fired."

This surprised Ron. However the threat of job loss provided strong extrinsic motivation to change. We developed a list of behaviors that were unacceptable. The question of disclosure was raised. I told Ron that he could request accommodations, but learning to control his temper was his responsibility.

Step 4: Take Action

A plan is meaningless until an individual follows through with action. To increase the likelihood of this happening:

- Explain *why* the actions are important.

- Check in to be sure the person isn't overwhelmed ("Is this the right amount to do, too much or not enough?").

- Ask what could get in the way and create a contingency plan.

- Ask how the person will remember what needs to be done.

- Check for understanding ("Let's review what you will do to update your résumé").

- Explain that if things go wrong, it simply indicates a need to re-strategize.

COMMUNICATION TOOLS

John and I were discussing his phobia of talking on the telephone.

"I don't like answering the phone at home," he said. "My mother gets mad when I say that she is reading a book."

"What do you mean?" I asked.

"Her friends call, and they ask, 'Is your mother there?' My mom shakes her head no. I say, 'She's reading a book,' and then my mother gets mad at me."

Oh goody! A social skills learning moment, I thought. I patiently explained why John's mother was not happy with John's response.

"If the caller knows that your mother is home but she'd rather read a book than talk, it might hurt the caller's feelings," I explained.

I silently congratulated myself for so deftly elucidating the concept.

"*My* feelings would not be hurt," John broke in, "and I will not lie to my mother's friends!"

So much for the lesson in pragmatics. Eventually we settled on a reply that would satisfy everyone: "I'm not sure that she can come to the phone. Let me check."

I include this vignette as another reminder of how profoundly communication deficits impact people on the autism spectrum. An activity as basic as answering the telephone is confusing. Little wonder that employment poses such a hurdle!

The tools that I describe in this section are ones that I use frequently in my practice. They have helped clients improve their communication skills in the workplace. However, it takes a lot of practice to internalize these skills and apply them in real situations. My clients vary in their ability to master these techniques. Progress must be measured based on the individual's improvement, not a neurotypical's standard of ability. I have seen motivated clients make significant progress and turn around difficult job situations.

Clients and I spend a lot of time "dissecting" interpersonal situations in order to:

- understand the context of an interaction

- make educated guesses about what the other person(s) knew, intended or expected

- figure out nonverbal signals that communicated knowledge, intention or expectation

- assess the effectiveness of the client's response

- determine how the response was interpreted by another

- learn how to better respond in the future.

When an individual's needs exceed what can be achieved in coaching, a referral should be made to a speech–language pathologist, psychologist or other clinician.

Small Talk and Basic Communication

The ability to exchange pleasantries with an interviewer and engage with co-workers is a basic and necessary skill. Aspergians struggle with small talk because they do not think of it as a way to establish and maintain relationships. They view communication as an information exchange. Again and again, clients ask me why they have to bother commenting about the weather or feigning interest in television programs that they have never seen.

Initially, it might seem trivial to worry about small talk. However, imagine that you are meeting a job candidate for an interview. You shake hands and introduce yourselves. You ask the candidate to follow you to your office where you will conduct the interview.

Scenario 1: You ask the candidate, "Did you have any trouble getting here?"
He answers, "No."
"Would you like anything to drink?"
"No."
The trip continues in silence. You reach your office and say, "Have a seat." The candidate sits down and looks at you, stone-faced.

Scenario 2: You ask the candidate, "Did you have any trouble getting here?"

He answers, "I got lost! The directions on your website are terrible! It says to make a right at the second light onto Crescent Street, but there is no sign for Crescent. I kept driving until I reached the end of Route 101. Then I had to turn around and come all the way back to the traffic light. I stopped in the Acme Mini Mart to ask for directions. I had to wait in line behind three other people. I asked the clerk where Crescent Street is, and she pointed across the street. That is why I was 10 minutes late. It wasn't my fault."

You clear your throat and say, "I didn't realize that the sign was down. I'm glad that you made it. Would you like something to drink?"

"Yes, a dark roast coffee with a touch of heavy cream."

My guess is that in both cases, the interview would be over in about ten minutes.

Aspergians are often anxious about making small talk because they do not know what to say. Or, they worry about saying the wrong thing and upsetting others. Some simply consider it absurd to ask about a co-worker's plans for the weekend when they have no interest in the other employee's activities.

Patricia was a data entry clerk and wanted to have better relationships with her co-workers. Several women in her department took an afternoon break together in the employee lounge. We decided that this was an opportunity for Patricia to practice friendly conversation.

We had already covered the basics of joining a conversation: approach the group, watch for acknowledgment of your presence, listen to the discussion, ask a question or make a comment related to the topic. We practiced how close to stand to others, smiling, exchanging greetings, and how to tell if one was not welcome to join a discussion.

One afternoon, Patricia saw three of her colleagues conversing in the lounge. She positioned herself near the group as she made herself some tea. She established eye contact, and when one woman asked, "How are you?" Patricia said, "Fine."

She listened to the discussion, waiting for a chance to join in. Then Patricia blurted out, "Why is the wall uneven?"

"Huh?" asked a co-worker. "What do you mean?"

"There is a picture missing from the wall," Patricia explained, "and now the others look uneven."

Patricia became aware of an uncomfortable silence. The co-worker said, "I don't know," and the women resumed their conversation. Patricia felt hurt that she was left out.

"Why do you think your co-workers reacted like that?" I asked.

"They always ignore me," she said, "they don't like me."

"What were they talking about?" I asked.

"Oh, something to do with a computer that crashed," she said. "Someone's work was lost and had to be done over."

"So they were talking about a broken computer and you mentioned a missing picture," I said. "I think they were confused because your question didn't have anything to do with what they were talking about. You suddenly changed the topic."

After thinking about my words for a few seconds, Patricia saw her mistake. She faced a common conundrum. She wanted to have friends at work, but she had to force herself to be interested in what they talked about.

This is how I break down the elements of small talk for a client:

- Small talk is a brief, back-and-forth exchange. People trade questions and comments about neutral topics, such as the weather, sports, traffic, a national news item or someone's plans for the weekend. The purpose is to show that you are interested in another person, not to exchange information. People usually take three or four turns asking questions or making comments.

- Watching the news or reading news summaries on the Internet is one way to find topics to that others will be familiar with.

- If people are talking about a subject that is unfamiliar, you can participate by asking a question to learn more (e.g. "I didn't hear about the accident on the Interstate. What happened?").

- Avoid controversial topics such as politics, religion, sex and gossip about other employees.

- Avoid observations about a person's weight, clothing, hair style, mannerisms or other personal attributes.

When a client is very uncomfortable engaging in this type of conversation, I'll practice with him. I name three of my personal interests, and ask him to choose one to discuss. We might need to work out exactly what questions or comments he will make before having the exchange. An assignment would be for him to come up with four or five questions or comments about one of my other interests, so we can practice at the next session.

The clients who seem the most uneasy often surprise me at their next coaching session by complimenting my jewelry, or inquiring about one of my hobbies.

Social Thinking® is a methodology developed by Michelle Garcia Winner and her colleague, Pamela Crooke, for teaching social skills to individuals who do not learn them intuitively. The Social Thinking Web site (www.socialthinking.com) contains articles and information about various products designed for children and adults. I frequently recommend *Social Thinking at Work, Why Should I Care?* (Winner and Crooke 2011) to my clients. I may assign reading and then work with a client to practice the concept.

Worksheets! for Teaching Social Thinking and Related Skills (Winner 2005) contains exercises on how to make and be part of a group, as well as perspective taking, understanding emotions and more. Worksheets that provide specific examples of how to start and maintain conversations are helpful for individuals who struggle to grasp the basics. (The worksheets in this book cover an age range from child to adult.)

A valuable resource for very high-functioning individuals is *How to Start a Conversation and Make Friends* (Gabor 2001). This book is written for neurotypicals and is suitable for clients who not need explicit instruction in communication basics.

Social Literacy, A Social Skills Seminar for Young Adults with ASDs, NLDs, and Social Anxiety (Cohen 2011) is based on the Social Skills Seminar developed at the University of Pennsylvania. The book and accompanying CD-ROM provide a 12-week course that is designed to be used with a group. I have successfully applied some of the strategies to my individual clients.

"Field" Observation

A direct and concrete method for learning about social norms of the workplace is observing co-workers. I position this as a "stealth" mission where a client quietly and unobtrusively observes how others interact in various situations.

Extroverted Ian learned that it was not okay to shout hellos to co-workers across the room or down the hall. Now he wanted to know whether it was acceptable to quietly greet each passerby. His assignment was to watch how his co-workers reacted when their colleagues walked past. We chose three busy times of day and set an observation period of ten minutes each. Ian was to stay at his desk and, in this case, mostly listen to what happened.

After two or three days of scrutiny, it was quite clear to Ian that greeting passersby was not a customary behavior. He made his own realization that it would be disruptive. Over the next few months, Ian began to spontaneously monitor how the people around him behaved in meetings, during breaks, at lunch and in other scenarios. He started matching his behavior to theirs.

Tamara asked too many questions in meetings.

"I'm ashamed!" she exclaimed. "Yesterday in a meeting my boss said, 'Other people have questions, too.'" She also noticed that a co-worker made a gesture, but she could not recall what it was or what it might have meant.

Tamara explained that she became distracted and "antsy" during meetings, which caused her inquisitiveness. One of her assignments was to discreetly take notes about how co-workers acted during meetings. In particular, Tamara was to observe who asked questions, how many, on what topics and when.

We also agreed that, for the coming two weeks, Tamara would limit her questions to two per meeting. She would write them down before asking, and allow at least two other people to make inquiries before raising hers.

Tamara wrote detailed notes about these assignments and put them into the front of a portfolio that she brought to meetings.

She made several important observations. People allowed a speaker to finish before asking questions. They almost always asked one question, and no more than two. She realized that when she allowed a speaker to finish, her questions were usually answered. And because this exercise forced her to pay closer attention during meetings, she was not compelled to ask multiple questions. At two meetings, she did not ask any at all.

Field observation encourages individuals to be aware of social interactions within the workplace and adapt their behavior accordingly to fit within the group.

When utilizing field observation, be sure that:

- The individual is clear on what he is observing, and when, where and for how long he will do this.

- Stealth observations are made. Discuss specifically how he will gather information without others knowing they are being watched. Be certain he understands that observation does not mean hiding, eavesdropping or following people around.

- The observation period is manageable and there is a plan for writing down what he notices.

Managing the Perception of Others

As previously discussed, Aspergians often have little awareness of the cause–effect relationship between their actions and how others perceive and treat them. Clients are typically quite surprised when I explain that they can influence these perceptions.

The process involves three questions:

- How do you want your co-workers/supervisor to perceive you?

- What can you do so that they will recognize you in that way?

- What do you need to stop doing?

The first question can shift a client into problem solving mode when he is agitated or perseverating on his difficulties. Beth irritated people by repeatedly asking basic questions. It upset her when co-workers said, "We already answered that," or "Look it up," or "You shouldn't have to ask that by now." Beth acknowledged that she *did* know how to answer most of the questions, or could find the answer on her own. The questioning was her impulsive reaction to anxiety.

Relating another incidence of annoyed co-workers and how this upset her, Beth was close to tears. Then I broke in and asked, "How do you want people to perceive you?"

Beth was silent.

"We've already talked about what your co-workers think when you ask the same question over and over," I prompted.

"They think that I am not listening," Beth said.

"Right, and that is annoying," I said. "How would you like them to perceive you instead?"

"I want them to think that I know what I am doing."

"Okay. In order for your co-workers to see you as a competent professional, what do you need to do differently?" I asked.

"Stop asking so many questions," Beth said. "Look things up for myself."

Managing perceptions by changing her behavior was a novel idea to her, and one that Beth was eager to implement. I explained that it would require consistent action over a reasonable period of time.

Beth tracked her progress in a log and over several weeks showed marked improvement. She also noticed other things that she could do to demonstrate professionalism, such as being less emotional in the workplace.

The process was more challenging for Kyle, who had recently earned an associate's degree. With the assistance of an on-site job coach, he was able to complete an internship. Now he wanted to find paid work.

Kyle's insistence on using military time (e.g. "I start at 0900 hours") probably confused other people. His habit of making random chirping sounds raised eyebrows during his internship.

Our discussions about proper workplace etiquette were not going well. Kyle knew what to do, but didn't want to change. Then his mother mentioned that, since graduating, Kyle considered himself a grown up instead of a student. He was very eager to get a job and earn money.

Grasping this motivational hook, I brought up a critical point.

"Kyle, we should talk about how to show that you are a grown up at work," I said, noticing that I had his full attention at the words *grown up*.

"What do you mean?" Kyle asked.

I decided to address the chirping first.

"Adults don't make chirping sounds at work," I said.

"Woof," said Kyle.

"They don't bark like dogs, either," I replied.

"Ribbit."

Somehow managing to stifle a laugh, I said, "Chirping, barking and frogs 'ribbit-ing' make me think of cartoons that children watch. Would you want people you work with to think you watch cartoons?"

Kyle gave me a long look and said, "Oink."

"Really, Kyle?" I asked, using my best teacher's voice. *Please don't moo*, I thought, *or I will lose it*. I watched and waited.

"Okay," he said, finally. "I get it."

Making the switch from military to civilian time turned out to be a battle.

"My father was in the army. He taught me military time," Kyle said.

"It makes sense that your father used military time, because all of the people he interacted with did the same thing," I said. "Using military time in a business office creates confusion, because other people won't understand what you mean."

"All you do is add 12 to the time when it's past noon," Kyle explained.

"But other people don't know that," I said.

"It's easy! If it's 2:00, you add 12, then it's 1400 hours," he said.

"People in an office refer to civilian time. If they want to have a meeting at 2:00 in the afternoon, they state that as 2:00pm," I explained.

"I'll tell them to add 12, and then it's 1400 hours," Kyle insisted.

"Do you see that you are asking other people to do a lot of work converting to military time?" I asked.

"It's not hard. All you do is add 12," he repeated.

If I smack myself on the forehead, I wonder if he would know that I am losing patience.

"I know that it's not hard," I said, "but it confuses people and makes them wonder why you won't fit into the group. From now on when we set coaching appointments, I will only listen if you tell me standard time."

It took several weeks and repeated challenges from Kyle, but I held my ground. He stopped using military time, at least in my presence. Woof!

The *Behavior Change Worksheet* (Worksheet 7.1) guides individuals through the process of changing how they are perceived in the workplace. Some clients need assistance to answer the questions.

Assign Reading of Management Books

At first, this may sound like a poor assignment. However, clients who work in corporations, or professionals such as physicians or lawyers, are expected to utilize advanced communication skills. These include negotiating, influencing, compromising and persuading.

With these clients, I use books written for business managers to develop a mini curriculum. A client completes some reading, and then we decide what techniques he will implement. I find the following books to be helpful for this purpose:

- *Successful Executive's Handbook, Development Suggestions for Today's Executives* (ePredix 1999)

- *Successful Manager's Handbook* (PreVisor and Personnel Decisions 2010)

- *Skills for New Managers* (Stettner 2000)

- *Working with Emotional Intelligence* (Goleman 1998).

Worksheet 7.1

BEHAVIOR CHANGE WORKSHEET

Your behavior influences the way that you are perceived in the workplace. Your supervisor and co-workers form impressions of you based on how you act. How they treat you is based on those impressions. For example, a person who interrupts will be perceived as rude and other people will avoid working with him or her.

Your goal in the workplace is to behave in ways that will be perceived as professional and courteous. Use this worksheet to increase your awareness of how a problem behavior affects your co-workers, and what you can do to change their impression of you.

1. Briefly describe the problem behavior:

   _____

   _____

2. How do others react when you engage in this behavior?

   _____

3. How do they treat you as a result?

   _____

4. How do you want others to perceive you?

   _____

5. How does your behavior need to change so that you are perceived positively?

   _____

   _____

6. When you are making a good impression on others, how will your work life be better?

   _____

   _____

Regulating Emotional Reactions

Individuals who have trouble controlling expressions of frustration, anger, anxiety or sadness put their jobs at risk. Emotional outbursts are disruptive and unsettling to co-workers. The individual may be judged as immature, mentally unstable or even dangerous. In most companies there is little or no tolerance of this type of behavior.

Aspergians may not be able to distinguish degrees of emotion using words. A person might not know how to differentiate irritation from annoyance, anger or rage. The use of a scale (e.g. "volume control," "emotional thermometer") enables a person to visually rank his degree of emotional arousal (Attwood 2007, p.135).

A scale can also show an individual when he is over-reacting to events and how to respond in an appropriate way. Contrasting a person's reaction to the seriousness of the situation is one way to do this (Crooke and Winner 2011, p.40). I set up a simple ten-point scale and divide it into segments. A minor situation might fall within the range of 1 to 3. A moderate situation would be in the range of 4 to 6. A serious situation would fall between 7 and 8. Points 9 and 10 designate catastrophic events.

I ask a client to place a current situation onto the scale. I do not judge his selection. Then we look for examples that belong at different points. Suppose that there is a conflict with a co-worker that the client rates as a level 5. I ask him for an example of a conflict that would rate at level 1–3. We repeat this with examples of level 7–8 and 9–10 conflicts. It may take a while to go through this step. A client might decide to revise his original ranking of the current event after completing this process.

Once we establish the seriousness of the situation, the individual rates his reaction to it. This rating can be based on how he actually responded or is planning to respond. We can then evaluate whether his reaction is in proportion to the gravity of the event.

This is an example of how the process works.

Scott became angry when colleagues challenged his ideas. He interpreted their questions or disagreement as a personal attack. Colleagues described his reactions as "explosive." Sometimes, Scott would storm out of a meeting. His supervisor made it clear that if Scott could not control his anger he would be fired.

During a coaching session, we used a ten-point scale to rate the seriousness of various scenarios where Scott had been challenged. For example:

- others doubting feasibility of a process he developed: 6 (high moderate)

- team members missing deadlines: 7 (serious)

- being asked several questions in quick succession: 8 (very serious)

- co-worker not responding to email on the day it was sent: 3 (minor).

Next, we examined how Scott reacted to each event. When one of his emails was "ignored," Scott sent another message asking why there had not been a response. If he happened to see the offender in the hallway he would ask, "Didn't you read my email?"

After much discussion, he rated this response as a "level 6 reaction to a level 3 problem."

"What would a level 3 reaction be?" I asked.

Scott said, "Wait a day or two and send a reminder. Or, if a situation is urgent, call the person on the telephone."

Scott's reaction to what he described as "rapid fire questioning" was typical of Aspergians. He could not process multiple questions in rapid succession. This caused his anxiety to rise and he would shut down. When a co-worker pressed him for a response, he would lose control and "explode."

Scott knew that even if the situation felt like a level 8, he needed to react at level 5 or less. After some experimentation, Scott discovered that he could diffuse these situations. He would ask co-workers to email him their questions, or say that he needed to think about them and would reply at a later time.

A rating scale helped Stephanie manage her anxiety at work. She admitted the tendency to catastrophize ("My therapist says I do that all the time"). In this agitated state, she was quick to lose patience with both her projects and co-workers.

We made a list of the situations that caused Stephanie to feel anxious or to panic:

- unsure of what to do

- frustration

- boredom

- anticipating a bad experience

- distracting noises

- other people close by

- being too cold in the office

- concern about getting fired

- hunger

- lack of motivation.

Next, Stephanie ranked them in order of severity on a 1 to 10 scale. The results looked like this:

Level 10 (catastrophic): Getting fired

Level 9:

Level 8:

Level 7:

Level 6:

Level 5: Unsure of what to do; anticipating a bad experience

Level 4: Frustration; other people close by

Level 3: Hunger; distracting noises

Level 2: Boredom; lack of motivation

Level 1 (most minor): Being too cold

Stephanie was surprised to see the scale.

"Most of these are not very serious," she said.

"From what you have described, it seems that you panic over minor situations, or normal experiences such as feeling bored once in a while," I said.

Stephanie was able to acknowledge that she was unlikely to be fired. We found too much evidence to the contrary: five years of employment; positive performance reviews; two raises.

"Which situation do you want to work on next?" I asked.

"I don't like being hungry every day," she said. "That makes me impatient."

Stephanie was hungry because she took her lunch break at 2:15pm.

"When it's over, I only have two more hours of work," she explained.

We went through the pros and cons of this strategy, and found several alternatives to help her better manage the workday. She decided to experiment by taking lunch from 12:15pm to 1:15pm each day for one week. This would be followed with a break at 3:15pm each afternoon. (For reasons I never learned, she preferred to schedule breaks at one quarter past the hour.)

In the interest of building momentum, I asked whether Stephanie next wanted to tackle being cold in the office. It was a minor concern and an easy fix. Or so I thought.

"What could you do to keep warm when the air conditioning makes your space too cold?" I began.

"I could wear one of my winter sweaters," she said, "but the wool would make my arms itch. All of my summer blouses have short sleeves."

"What about buying a cotton sweater to wear in the summertime?" I replied.

"I could try wearing a sweater. But what if I get too warm?" she asked.

"You could take it off," I countered.

"But then my arms would be cold," she said.

"How can you solve the problem of your arms being cold when you wear short-sleeved blouses at work?" I asked.

This was not the first such discussion that I'd had with Stephanie, or some of my other clients.

"I could buy long-sleeved blouses," Stephanie said, "but then I'd have to go to a department store and I hate shopping!"

"How worth it would it be to spend a couple of hours shopping in order to be more comfortable every day at work?" I wondered.

Stephanie looked at me, and then smiled.

"I'm being resistant, aren't I?" she said.

"Yes," I agreed, "and I wonder if it's because you are starting to feel overwhelmed."

Changing her lunch routine was enough for Stephanie to do in the coming week.

The subject of sweaters and long-sleeved blouses didn't come up again. However, over the next few months Stephanie made other improvements. She got permission to use a white noise machine in her cubicle, and began asking for help when she wasn't sure of how to complete a task.

She was also able to put some of her emotional reactions into better perspective. It hadn't occurred to her that co-workers could feel emotions, but not show or talk about them.

Perspective Taking Using Reporter's Questions

The "Five W" reporter's questions provide a framework for anticipating social interactions and preparing how to cope with them. Here is an example of how the questions can be used:

- *What is the purpose of the gathering:* company meeting, formal department meeting, informal staff lunch, holiday party?

- *Who will be present:* everyone in the company, supervisor, peers, the CEO?

- *Why are they there:* company-wide announcement, update project status, socialize?

- *Where is the event:* at the office; a restaurant, supervisor's office, conference room?

- *When does it take place:* during business hours, at lunch time, in the evening, on the weekend, all day, for two hours?

A reorganization at Leslie's company resulted in layoffs and the appointment of a new general manager. Leslie knew that she had to "put in face time" at the upcoming holiday party. She was extremely uncomfortable at such events. Using the Five Ws, Leslie planned a strategy:

- travel to the venue with other department members

- stay for 30 to 45 minutes

- have a soft drink and something to eat

- stick close to co-workers; pretend to be interested in conversations

- say hello to her supervisor and the new general manager

Daniel and I used the Five Ws to prepare for a co-worker's birthday celebration. We established that:

- the gathering will be brief, approximately 30 minutes

- cake and soft drinks will be served, possibly other snacks, too

- he was not expected to bring a gift

- attendees would not wear party hats

- he should have one piece of cake only

- he should not ask to bring leftovers home

- even though it was a celebration, work rules applied ("I can't get too giddy")

- usual work dress applied.

At his next coaching session, Daniel reported that he did not dominate the celebration, ate a second piece of cake because it was offered to him, and that "No one got mad at me."

Mentor or "Work Buddy"

In every organization, there are unique procedures, policies and reporting structures that can only be learned on the job, from other employees. Finding a mentor or "work buddy" can be very helpful for someone with Asperger's Syndrome. This is a colleague (not a supervisor or human resources representative) who is either a designated mentor or simply a friendly peer.

The buddy can translate unspoken workplace rules, such as what the real priorities are, how a supervisor prefers to receive information, who is trustworthy and not. He can explain the ever-elusive office politics. A mentor or work buddy can also:

- offer advice on how to complete tasks more efficiently

- provide "reality checks" (e.g. is a supervisor critical of everyone, or just him; are others confused by the new software; does everyone have too much work?).

An individual may not be able to establish this type of relationship on his own. Mentoring can be requested as an accommodation (see Chapter 8 for information on disclosure and accommodations).

I have had a number of cases where a client was able to significantly improve performance thanks to the guidance of a knowledgeable and willing co-worker.

EXECUTIVE FUNCTION TOOLS

Some individuals with Asperger's Syndrome are extremely well organized. However, most struggle to manage information and perform tasks efficiently. A few well-chosen organizational or time management tools may address problems. Or, a person may need to find a job with fewer executive function demands.

Based on my experience, I categorize executive function challenges as follows:

- understanding expectations (What do I need to do?)
  - purpose of a task
  - what the finished product should look like
  - getting started and staying motivated
- planning (How will I do it?)
  - determining the steps
  - creating a schedule
- managing time efficiently (When is it due?)
  - estimating how long tasks will/should take
  - prioritizing
  - staying on track
- solving problems (What could go wrong?)
  - being flexible
  - seeing options
  - staying calm
  - asking for help
  - following through (What action must I take?).

CLIENT PORTRAIT: KAREN'S EXECUTIVE FUNCTION NIGHTMARE

Karen was employed for over three years as an assistant archivist at a large academic institution. Her job was to scan photographs and documents into an electronic database and fulfill information requests from various departments. The university was developing a more sophisticated archival system that could store a voluminous amount of historical data, as well as student, faculty and administrative staff records. The project would take several years to complete.

Prior to joining the university, Karen, who was in her early 30s, had several jobs that she did not find particularly interesting or challenging. She was terminated from a receptionist position because she didn't smile at customers. She left a retail job of her own volition because interacting with customers was too stressful. For several years, she was an administrative assistant at a small medical practice. While there, she enrolled in a certificate program to learn archivism. One of the instructors helped her get the job at the university.

Karen had recently been promoted to manager. In her new role, she helped to create a complex database for archiving data. An integral part of the process was maintaining a large spreadsheet that categorized the many types of documents, and how they should be filed. Employees in the information technology group used this information to build the archival system.

However, just three months after the promotion, Karen was placed on probation. Her supervisor complained that she made too many errors and that critical tasks were not completed on time. According to her boss, Karen was only performing "20 percent of the job." This shocked and confused Karen.

When Karen contacted me her goal was to save her job. Specifically, she wanted to address her supervisor's concerns and end her probationary status. She needed help to figure out what job accommodations she would need.

Karen was diagnosed with Asperger's Syndrome in college. She described life-long difficulties with organization and completing tasks. Specifically she had difficulty:

- prioritizing

- judging how long projects would take

- figuring out ambiguous tasks

- meeting deadlines

- interacting with too many different people.

Shortly after she joined the university, Karen disclosed her Asperger's to the human resources manager and to her supervisor.

I asked Karen to make a list of the pros and cons of her current position. It looked like this:

Pros	Cons
• Job is challenging; engages my intellect	• Supervisor is intense and task driven
• Not bored during the day	• Pressure to perform
• Like most of my co-workers	• Don't understand how other departments will use the archiving system
• No set schedule: can take breaks and lunch when I want	• Don't know the purpose of certain tasks
	• Don't know which tasks are critical
	• Hard to manage time
	• Don't know how long tasks should take
	• Not sure of priorities
	• Two month backlog of emails
	• Anxious about asking for help

I noted the imbalance between the two columns. It was also intriguing to me that Karen placed so much importance on the flexible schedule, particularly her freedom to choose her lunch hour. She mentioned it several times during our sessions. A number of items in the second column seemed to be integral parts of her job.

There were other red flags.

As manager, Karen attended five to six staff meetings per week. Being around others made her anxious. She had trouble simultaneously listening and writing, so she did not take notes. She forgot what she heard and left meetings unsure of what she was expected to do. Since she did not know what to prepare, she was taken off guard by questions. Karen was embarrassed to learn from her boss that a particular spreadsheet was a critical component of the archiving project. "I don't know what needs to be done, or why it's important," she said.

Karen did not work from a schedule. She would forget tasks or realize at the last minute that she would miss a deadline. Her co-workers complained that she asked the same question again and again. Karen explained that she would forget the answer.

Karen had been promoted into an executive function nightmare. Still, she believed that with modifications she could meet performance expectations. She presented the following accommodation requests to her supervisor and a human resources representative:

- twice weekly meetings with her supervisor to discuss priorities, the best way to handle tasks and how to be more efficient

- explanations of why she was performing certain tasks

- assignments given in writing, not verbally

- ability to review meeting notes taken by a colleague

- help from a co-worker to organize her files and workspace.

Karen reported that her boss did not say much during this meeting.

Additionally, Karen agreed to do several things. She would create a monthly project schedule and weekly to-do list, and review these with her supervisor. She would also develop check lists of procedures for multi-step tasks.

Three weeks after requesting the accommodations, Karen's supervisor decided that Karen could not manage the core responsibilities of the job. "At the manager level," she explained, "you need to handle most of these tasks independently." Karen was demoted to her previous position of assistant archivist.

Karen was understandably upset by this news. She had done the very best that she could to perform the job satisfactorily. She believed that her boss should have been more patient and helped her more.

"This was my chance to have a job that was interesting and challenging, and I blew it," she said.

"You were promoted because you do very good work," I said. "In this case, you were given a job that emphasizes tasks that are difficult, instead of what you do well."

It was unfortunate that Karen accepted the position without really understanding what it involved. Had she been able to shadow the former manager (who was promoted), she might have realized that the job was not a good fit. Or she could have requested accommodations from the start.

Karen found herself in a job that would be extremely hard for anyone with executive function deficits to handle, with:

- complex, long-term projects

- many tasks to plan, prioritize and monitor simultaneously

- tight deadlines

- significant amount of interaction with others

- shifting between big picture strategic decisions and execution of detailed tasks.

Karen's priority was now to find a career that would be more enjoyable.

She took the SDS assessment (see Chapter 5) and scored zero in the category of Enterprising. She showed strong preferences in the categories of Artistic and Conventional. Karen affirmed that she did not want a job that involved launching projects, championing ideas or leading other people. She liked working by herself and enjoyed writing. She wondered whether there were careers that would utilize her writing talent and provide the structure she needed.

Karen also completed a self-assessment of her important work criteria and ideal work environment. She wanted a job that provided:

- lots of structure

- daily routine

- orderly, relaxed pace

- minimal interaction with others

- work involving facts and information

- low stress.

The assessments helped to change Karen's perspective. She realized that the manager's job was unsuitable and no longer felt upset that it didn't work out. "As assistant archivist, I know what needs to be done," she said. "There is structure, and not a lot of pressure. When I was manager, I was working late every day and would come home exhausted from all of the stress."

She realized that she had options and could find work that was a better fit. Karen decided to stay at the university while she explored other occupations.

Understanding Expectations

Individuals with Asperger's Syndrome have trouble inferring expectations and translating abstract directives such as "run the numbers." In my workshops, I explain to professionals and employers that they need to make "The Obvious" obvious to a person with Asperger's Syndrome.

This should not be done by asking, "Do you understand what to do?" The individual may become defensive or say "yes," believing that he knows how to proceed, when this is not the case. Instead, expectations should be clarified by:

- explaining the purpose of a task or project

- providing clear start and end points

- providing samples or examples of the finished product

- supplying templates

- requesting an outline or sample when a project is new or complex

- reviewing work in stages

- quantifying productivity requirements whenever possible

- assigning due dates

- stating priorities.

The individual should be told to ask questions if he is not sure of what is expected.

Planning

A client may need assistance in determining the steps required to complete a project or task. Otherwise, he will become frustrated and overwhelmed and do nothing. The steps should be written down and assigned due dates when necessary.

In addition to planning a specific activity, he may need a system for prioritizing and planning various workday tasks. Increasingly, I find myself recommending that clients plan out their work week using paper appointment books. Unlike electronic organizers, the planners provide a clear visual of commitments for the week.

I do not assume that a person will know how to create a workable schedule. Tracy was attempting to coordinate her work schedule with her children's after school activities. Her initial plan was to purchase two planners: one for work and one for personal time. When we discussed how she would coordinate entries in two separate appointment books, Tracy saw that they system would be complicated. She was happy with my suggestion that she use one planner and different colored ink for work and family commitments.

You should also determine how the individual will remember to look at his schedule since Aspergians are notoriously forgetful. Some clients have crafted comprehensive plans only to forget all about them!

There can be unexpected complications in planning for some individuals.

Jack was practicing interviewing skills. He was tired of his retail job and wanted to work in an office. He sent several résumés in response to openings for data entry clerks. We made a list of the questions he might be asked, and brainstormed how to answer them. Jack was diligent about practicing his responses, and did well in our role play.

He was concerned about fitting interviews into his schedule.

"I can't set up many interviews, because my work schedule changes every week," he said.

Employees at the retail store received their hours for the coming week on Friday afternoons. Jack was confused about a conversation he had with an employer who wanted to interview him for a data entry opening.

"She asked whether I could come in for an interview next Wednesday," he said.

"What did you say?" I asked.

"I don't know."

That was all he said. The employer asked again whether he could come in on Wednesday.

"I said that I won't know my hours until Friday, and told her to call me back," he explained.

He was surprised that he didn't receive another call.

We arranged a contingency plan. If Jack was contacted about an interview prior to a Friday, he would say, "I will know my schedule for next week on Friday. Can I call you then to schedule an interview?"

A few weeks later, Jack was hired by an insurance company to perform data entry.

Managing Time Efficiently

When a client is struggling to manage assignments and meet deadlines, I ask him to do a quick self-assessment. I want to know whether he:

- adds unnecessary time to projects by striving for perfection

- spends long periods of time trying to solve problems on his own

- insists on doing things a certain way, when others have suggested short cuts

- starts every project from scratch

- continually underestimates how long a task will take

- spends too much time on low-priority tasks.

Almost always, the person engages in at least one of these productivity killers. He typically has no idea of how he spends his time during the day. There is little incentive to make changes, or he doesn't know how to change.

For this reason I ask a client to track how he is spending his time using a simple log (see Worksheet 7.2). For one or two weeks, he notes how long he spent on various activities. He also rates their importance using this legend: C = Critical (had to be done today); I = Important (specific deadline); L = Low priority (do when there is time).

My clients are usually surprised when they review their logs. They see that too much time is spent on unessential activities or the wrong priorities. Sometimes, just filling out the log becomes a big project. I have learned to reassure clients that they do not have to account for *every* minute of their workday. Nor do they have to precisely account for time ("You can round 13 minutes up to 15").

Leanne arrived at her coaching session clutching five days' worth of log sheets. Before she sat down, she started telling me about problems.

"On Monday, I was answering emails when the telephone rang," she said. "I didn't pay attention to how much time I spent on emails and on my call, so I wasn't sure what to write down."

"That's okay," I replied, "you don't have to be exact. What's your best estimate of how long you spent doing both?"

"About 20 minutes," she said, fishing a pen out of her tote bag to revise her log. She looked up at me and said, "The log is divided into 15 minute-increments. Now what?"

"The purpose of this is to get a general idea of how you are spending your time," I said. "It is fine to write *emails and phone* in one 15-minute block."

"On Tuesday afternoon, I was so busy, I didn't have time to fill in the chart," Leanne continued. "My boss was out of town from Wednesday through Friday. What I have for these days isn't very accurate. When he's in town, I get called into a lot more meetings."

"I understand. We're looking for patterns. No two weeks are going to be the same," I said.

Next, we delineated "critical" and "important."

"I don't know how to rate this item," she said. "It was critical to the project. But I didn't *have* to do it on Thursday."

The experience of debriefing the log told me a lot about why Leanne had so much trouble managing her workload.

"I'm curious about what patterns you noticed about how you spend your time," I asked.

Leanne *was* able to identify one time drain: the numerous and detailed emails she exchanged with other people in her department. We verbally wrestled for 15 minutes until she agreed to try calling colleagues to discuss complex issues.

It is important that the individual becomes aware of his time drains. I ask him to make the decision about which one(s) he wants to address. Here is a sample of the daily log:

Worksheet 7.2

DAILY ACTIVITY LOG

Here is a sample of the daily log, which typically runs from 8:00am to 6:00pm.

Instructions: Copy this sheet for each business day over the next one or two weeks. Record your daily activities in 15-minute increments. If an activity lasts over 15 minutes, draw a vertical arrow to note its length. In the column marked Priority, indicate the urgency of each activity: C = Critical; I = Important; L = Low priority.

Time	Activity	Priority
8:00–8:15am	Respond to emails	I
8:15–8:30am		
8:30–8:45am		
8:45–9:00am		
9:00–9:15am		
9:15–9:30am		
9:30–9:45am		
9:45–10:00am		
10:00 –10:15am		

Another impediment to staying on schedule is underestimating how long tasks or projects will take. Even when an individual has done the same type of work for years, he may not be able to make accurate predictions. This is another example of reduced ability to generalize based on the big picture.

Teri had written technical manuals for nearly two decades. Previous employers agreed that the quality of her work was very good. Her problem was that she worked too slowly. When she was hired at another technology company, she began working with me, determined to be successful.

"My boss says that the manual must be completed in three weeks," she began, "but I have no idea whether I can meet that deadline."

Teri could not think back to similar projects from the past and use the information to make reasonable guesses in the present. Instead, she embarked on a terrifically inefficient process to figure out a schedule. Hours were spent laboriously looking through product specifications in an attempt to figure out how exactly how many diagrams and pages the document would contain. She showed me an elaborate spreadsheet that for all of its data didn't answer her fundamental question: how many pages would be in the manual?

She became sidetracked by the software program the company used to format the manuals.

"Learning this system will take time," she said. "The program I used at previous jobs was easy to use. I could get the manual done faster with it."

Several more hours had been devoted to comparing the two software programs. Teri even called the manufacturer of her preferred software to discuss pricing. She was planning to write a proposal recommending that her new company purchase the software.

"That would be an expensive undertaking," I observed. "Then the other writers would need to be trained on how to use it. How likely is it that the company will want to make that purchase?"

"Based on my research it would save everyone time," Teri replied.

"That might be true. But even if your supervisor wanted to make the change, it would take months before the software would be installed. Your deadline is three weeks away. Is this really a priority?"

"I guess not," Teri concluded.

Seeing the long and ineffectual system that Teri employed in an attempt to create a schedule made me think back to my days as a marketing manager. After a year of producing sales brochures, advertisements and direct mail packages, I developed a sense of the amount of time involved to do each one. I could create accurate project schedules with a minimum of effort. This is because I was able to:

- draw on my past experience creating similar marketing materials

- incorporate knowledge of the copywriting, graphic design and printing processes

- adjust schedules based on the turnaround times at current vendors

- make allowances for the preferences and work styles of the other people who were involved (remembering who approved projects quickly, and who always asked for revisions).

It didn't matter that each document was not *exactly* the same, or that different suppliers were involved. I generalized my knowledge and experience.

I showed Teri the *Estimating and Measuring Time to Complete Tasks* worksheet (Worksheet 7.3) and she agreed to try the approach. She wrote down each step involved in writing a manual. Then she made her best guess as to how long each step would take. Teri next had to monitor her progress as she worked on a step. At the halfway point, she was to check whether her estimate was accurate. For example, if Teri estimated that it would take her two hours to write one chapter, she should be about 50 percent finished after one hour.

Using this tool, Teri soon noticed a pattern. She was repeatedly only about one quarter of the way through a step at the halfway point. She saw that she underestimated the necessary time by 50 percent.

Teri used this template and got some help from a friendly colleague at work. She developed more realistic estimates of her writing speed, and planned her schedule accordingly.

When a client doesn't know how to make a reasonable time estimate, I suggest that he speak to his supervisor or a peer for advice.

Solving Problems (What could go wrong?)

The ability to solve problems is a skill that is used in many different jobs. It requires that an employee is flexible and able to deal with novel situations.

Problem solving involves a number of different skills. First, the problem must be accurately identified and defined. Next, a strategy must be developed to solve it. To do this, an employee must gather and organize relevant information that will help him determine the best solution.

Worksheet 7.3

ESTIMATING AND MEASURING TIME TO COMPLETE TASKS

1. Task: _____

   _____

2. Due date: _____

3. Steps and *estimated* time to complete

   Step 1: _____

   Estimated Time to Complete _____

   Step 2: _____

   Estimated Time to Complete _____

   Step 3: _____

   Estimated Time to Complete _____

   Step 4: _____

   Estimated Time to Complete _____

   Step 5: _____

   Estimated Time to Complete _____

   Total time: _____

4. Start task at _____(time)

   End task at _____(time)

5. At halfway point, my goal is to have the following amount of work completed:

   _____

6. *Actual* time to complete each step

    Step 1: _____

    Actual Time to Complete _____

    Step 2: _____

    Actual Time to Complete _____

    Step 3: _____

    Actual Time to Complete _____

    Step 4: _____

    Actual Time to Complete _____

    Step 5: _____

    Total time: _____

7. If the actual time to complete a step/task took longer than the estimated time, then:

    a. What obstacles, if any, did I not anticipate?

    _____

    b. How can I approach the task differently next time?

    _____

It is necessary to prioritize the seriousness of the problem so that decisions can be made about how much time, money and effort should be spent trying to resolve it. Once a solution is implemented, progress must be monitored and adjustments may need to be made. Finally, results are evaluated to see whether the solution was optimal (Cherry 2014b).

Individuals with Asperger's Syndrome typically have trouble developing realistic plans to solve problems they encounter in the workplace. There are several reasons for this. The individual may:

- misidentify what the real problem is

- misjudge its severity (over- or underestimate the seriousness)

- spend too much time on minor problems, or vice versa

- gather the wrong information, or too little or too much information to solve it

- insist on doing things in his own way; ignore advice or conventional wisdom

- repeat what hasn't worked in the past because he can't see options

- be unable to apply strategies from past situations to the present one

- have trouble weighing options and inferring likely results

- see the situation in all or nothing terms; be unable to compromise or make exceptions

- panic and act impulsively or ignore the situation

- lose sight of the big picture and make decisions based on the wrong data.

The *Problem Solving Action Plan* worksheet (Worksheet 7.4) helped Teri to realize that convincing her employer to purchase new software was unfeasible. The real problem was allocating enough time for her projects.

Tools like this are certainly helpful. However, it is also important to assess whether an individual is in the right job. Usually, the less structured the job, the more problem solving is required.

Worksheet 7.4

PROBLEM SOLVING ACTION PLAN

1. Describe the problem (briefly): _____

   _____

2. State your goal (desired outcome): _____

   _____

3. Define what is getting in the way of reaching your goal: _____

   _____

   _____

4. List possible solutions for each obstacle, and the pros and cons of each. Then rate the chances of success, using this scale:

   1. Not likely   2. Unsure

   3. Somewhat likely   4. Very likely

   Then, rate the cost or effort required to implement each solution, using this scale:

   1. Great cost/effort   2. Moderate cost/effort

   3. Little cost/effort   4. No cost/effort

   Solution A: _____

   Pros: _____

   Cons: _____

   Chance of success: _____ Cost/effort required to implement: _____

Solution B: _____

Pros: _____

Cons: _____

Chance of success: _____ Cost/effort required to implement: _____

Solution C: _____

Pros: _____

Cons: _____

Chance of success: _____ Cost/effort required to implement: _____

5. Which solution will you commit to trying? _____

    _____

6. How will you implement the solution? _____

    _____

7. How you will you track your progress? _____

    _____

There is one characteristic that I have observed in every person with Asperger's Syndrome who I have coached:

Aspergians are reluctant to ask for help.

There are several reasons why:

- concern about being considered "stupid"

- belief that since he was hired, he is expected to know everything about the job

- fear of being fired for asking the "wrong" question

- not knowing who or how to ask for help

- preferring to devise his own solution.

I stress to clients that asking for help, in the right way and at the right time, is the smart thing to do. I explain that one of the characteristics of a good executive is "knowing what you don't know" and finding people who have the answers.

A client may need specific assistance to determine who to ask and how to make his inquiries. His questions may not be appropriate for the workplace, such as how to make small talk or adequate eye contact. If he is asking too many questions, it may indicate a need for more training. When a question is repeated multiple times, it may be due to anxiety, or mean that he needs to make notes to remember what to do.

Establishing rules for who, how and when to ask is not as easy as it sounds. John had been assigned to a project that was more complex than usual. He was stressed, anxious and confused about certain tasks.

"It sounds like you need to ask you supervisor to explain the process," I said.

"I can't," replied John. "He said that I ask too many questions and need to figure things out for myself."

"But that was when you got nervous and asked basic questions. This is different. There are aspects of this project that are brand new," I said.

Due to his literalness, John thought that he should always try to figure out his own answers. It was extremely hard for him to grasp the difference between compulsively asking about routine matters and having a legitimate question.

Sometimes clients get into trouble for *being* too helpful. Frequently, Aspergians will point out grammatical or factual errors made by others. One man began doing tasks that were assigned to a co-worker because he believed that he did a better job!

Ben was a sales associate at a retail store. He noticed what appeared to be inefficiencies and began challenging his boss and the other associates about the procedures. "I thought they would be glad to know about a better way to do things," he said. In less than a month he was fired.

Following Through (Taking Action)

One of the barriers to successfully completing tasks is remembering what needs to be done. Aspergians often have weak short-term and working memory. They can easily forget tasks, instructions and deadlines.

These are helpful tips for individuals who are forgetful (some could be job accommodations):

- Find a quiet workspace where there will be limited interruptions; close the door or post a "do not disturb" sign outside a cubicle when working on an important task.

- Schedule two or three specific times per day to check voice- and email; turn off the email notification system on a computer.

- Wear noise-canceling headphones or use a white-noise machine if sounds are distracting.

- Create routines instead of relying on memory.

- Use check lists.

- Write things down immediately; carry a small pad for this purpose.

- Utilize electronic organizers.

- Use mnemonics to jog memory (e.g. rhymes or acronyms).

- "Chunk" information by grouping individual items into a whole.

I remind clients that anxiety, stress and fatigue make it harder to concentrate and remember information. Taking two or three short breaks during the day can make a big difference in performance. Regular exercise is also helpful.

Planning goals and action steps for the week, or a particular project, helps to focus attention and encourage follow through. When clients use the *Weekly Goals and Action Items* worksheet (Worksheet 7.5), we figure out where they can post it so that they will see it daily. The individual is asked to rate his satisfaction with his progress, which reinforces the need to monitor results.

Worksheet 7.5

WEEKLY GOALS AND ACTION ITEMS

For the week of: _____

Goal 1: _____

 Specific steps I will take toward this goal:

 a. _____

 b. _____

 c. _____

 d. _____

Goal 2: _____

 Specific steps I will take toward this goal:

 a. _____

 b. _____

 c. _____

 d. _____

Goal 3: _____

 Specific steps I will take toward this goal:

 a. _____

 b. _____

 c. _____

 d. _____

Progress

Goal	Action Steps Achieved?	Results
1:	a. yes no	_____ _____ _____ _____
2:	a. yes no	_____ _____ _____ _____
3:	a. yes no	_____ _____ _____ _____

My level of satisfaction with my progress this week:

☐ Very satisfied ☐ Somewhat satisfied ☐ Not satisfied

Chapter 8

DISCLOSURE AND WORKPLACE ACCOMMODATIONS

The protections offered by the Americans with Disabilities Act (ADA), and similar anti-discrimination laws in other countries, can mean the difference between an individual keeping and losing his job. The ADA prohibits employers from discriminating against individuals with disabilities. It requires companies to make reasonable accommodations, which are modifications that enable a person to participate in the interviewing process, or to perform his job.

It is outside the scope of this book to fully describe the ADA and the criteria for being considered disabled. Readers in the United States are encouraged to visit the Web site of the Job Accommodation Network (JAN) (http://askjan.org) for a detailed discussion of anti-discrimination laws. JAN is a service of the US Department of Labor's Office of Disability Employment Policy. Its Web site offers a wealth of information about the ADA, including guides with accommodation ideas for various disabilities. Readers in other countries should consult the appropriate government agency.

The information in this chapter will help you assist individuals in deciding whether, when and what to disclose, and how to request reasonable accommodations. It provides a basic description of the ADA, including points that are essential to know when developing a disclosure strategy.

In nearly all cases, the decision to disclose is the individual's. Deciding whether this is the right option depends on the nature of the job, the person's challenges and overall performance, and his comfort disclosing a disability.

There are risks to disclosing. A job offer could be rescinded, a promotion denied or a job lost without the real reason being stated. It can be difficult, expensive and time consuming to prove discrimination.

As stated in the Introduction, the fact that Asperger's Syndrome is no longer a diagnosis in the DSM raises particular concerns for those in mid-management or professional positions. Some of my clients worry that disclosing autism could negatively impact their careers. Many organizations require that an employee provide proof of a medical diagnosis. It will be interesting to see whether clinicians will continue to use terminology such as "Asperger's Syndrome (autism spectrum disorder)" to designate high-functioning individuals.

The ADA requires that an employer provides equal opportunities to *qualified* individuals at every stage of the employment cycle. This includes hiring, firing, promotions, compensation, training and benefits. A qualified individual is someone with the requisite education, skills, experience and ability. An employer does not have to lower quality or productivity standards for an employee who is disabled. If all data entry clerks are expected to enter 60 records per hour and Susan, who has Asperger's Syndrome, can only enter 47, she would be considered unqualified for the job.

The purpose of disclosing a disability is to request reasonable accommodation(s). An accommodation is a modification that enables a person to participate in the interviewing process, or to perform the essential functions of his job. The ADA compels an employer to make reasonable accommodations for qualified individuals with disabilities.

The modification must be realistic and cannot cause an undue hardship for the employer. The definition of what is reasonable depends on the company and the job. For data entry clerk Susan, requesting written instructions was reasonable. However, Ken worked as a financial analyst. His job required judgment. It was not possible to provide written instructions about how to address every possible situation.

Modifications that would incur significant cost or disrupt an aspect of the business would be considered an undue hardship for the employer. However, an undue hardship at a company with 25 employees might not be considered one at a company with 10,000 employees.

An employee with a disability must be able to perform the essential functions of his job, or he can be fired. *Essential job functions* are the core tasks and responsibilities for which the person was hired. For an accountant, using standard accounting software would be considered an essential function. An employee with visual-spatial processing problems, who could not use spreadsheets, would be considered unqualified for the position.

The law states that accommodations can include the reassignment of unessential tasks to another employee. Using spreadsheets would not be considered an essential job function for a copywriter who creates budgets once per year.

It is important to recognize that an individual requesting accommodation is negotiating with his employer. There is no official list of accommodations that an employer must grant. They are decided on a case-by-case basis. Further, an employer does not have to acquiesce to a specific request, and may offer an alternative accommodation instead.

The law is designed to protect the interests of both individuals and organizations. Individuals who approach the process ready for battle usually do not have a positive outcome. Threatening an employer with legal action should be avoided at all cost.

DISCLOSING IN A SOLUTION-FOCUSED WAY

A common mistake is to present a list of problems and expect an employer to find solutions. Most supervisors and human resources managers know little about Asperger's Syndrome. A statement such as, "I have Asperger's and can't multitask" puts the burden of accommodation on those who know the least about what is needed. Proactively suggesting reasonable solutions greatly increases the likelihood that they will be implemented.

I follow a three-step process for helping clients plan a disclosure strategy:

1. Determine *what* to disclose.

2. Decide *how* to disclose.

3. Choose *when* to disclose.

When determining what to disclose I ask a client to list every challenge he is facing on the job, or with submitting applications/interviewing. This reveals accommodation needs as well as any areas that the individual must change or develop on his own.

Next, we discuss how each challenge impacts the client's performance, and what accommodations he believes will enable him to meet expectations. For example:

Challenge	Impact	Accommodation
• Prioritizing	• Too much time on non-essential tasks • Misses deadlines	• Daily/weekly review with supervisor

The third step is planning how to make the disclosure. My clients often need assistance with this step. Some are extremely nervous about what to say. They may plan long, detailed explanations that include the history of Asperger's Syndrome and current research into its cause or manifestations. One man drafted a two-page letter to his new supervisor that included quotations from the *Diagnostic and Statistical Manual of Mental Disorders*. Not only did it contain many details that were irrelevant to the workplace, it is highly unlikely that his boss would understand terms like "restricted repetitive and stereotyped patterns of behavior."

Disclosure should be done in person and a human resources representative should be involved. It is a mistake to assume that managers understand the ADA or how to accommodate employees. Human resources personnel are trained in the law and also responsible for documenting accommodation requests.

Disclosing only to a supervisor could mean that legitimate accommodation requests are brushed aside. One of my clients was told, "It is not my responsibility to learn about your disability." Fortunately, the human resources department became involved and let the manager know that it was his responsibility.

The employee decides who in the organization may know about his disability. He is within his rights to request that human resources and his supervisor not mention it to anyone else. Or, he can name certain individuals with whom this information will be shared.

Disclosure statements should be brief and to the point, like Lesley's. She explained, "I have Asperger's Syndrome, a neurological condition that makes it hard for me to remember verbal instructions. During training, I need to make notes and practice the steps in order." Any verbal requests should be followed up in writing. A *brief* article about Asperger's Syndrome might accompany such requests.

I take time to carefully plan how a client will phrase his accommodation request. I discourage individuals from using phrases such as "poor social skills." This is extremely vague and hard to accommodate. It might suggest poor manners, disinterest in interacting with others or a personality problem. Be specific. An individual who explains that he is very literal can be accommodated by receiving explicit instructions.

The final step in the process is choosing when to disclose. There are pros and cons to disclosing at different stages of the employment cycle. The particular individual and his circumstances will also influence the timing.

The following are some pros and cons to consider:

Disclosing in a cover letter or when submitting a job application:

Makes sense when: the individual needs assistance filling out an application or participating in the interviewing process. Or, if having Asperger's Syndrome provides a distinct advantage, such as applying for a job at an autism association. Even then, the individual's skills and experience should be the primary focus.

Avoid when: no specific assistance is needed. Early-stage disclosure focuses attention on potential problems rather than a candidate's qualifications. Many employers are apprehensive about hiring people with disabilities. The fear is that they will need an inordinate amount of training or supervision, or require costly accommodations.[1] Another concern is being sued if an employee is terminated for not meeting performance requirements. This myth persists even though the ADA clearly spells out that employers are within their right to fire such employees.

Disclosing during a job interview:

Makes sense when: an individual's challenges are so noticeable or hard to control that not offering an explanation will disqualify him from consideration. Very slow processing speed or the inability to make adequate eye contact can appear to be cognitive impairment, disinterest or lack of preparation. A brief explanatory statement should be made.

Avoid when: a disability is not obvious. Whenever possible, the focus of an interview should be on the candidate's capabilities not his limitations or potential problems.

Disclosing after receiving a job offer:

Makes sense when: a significant accommodation will be needed immediately. In the United States, an employer cannot rescind a job offer because a disability is disclosed. Waiting until the first day on the job to reveal a significant accommodation need creates an atmosphere of distrust.

Avoid when: the individual believes that he can perform the job in a satisfactory manner. He always has the option of disclosing in the future, if accommodations become necessary.

---

1   According to a JAN study (*Workplace accommodations: Low cost, high impact*) more than half of accommodations cost nothing, and the rest cost $500 or less.

Disclosing after starting the job:

Makes sense when: there are significant performance problems. This is the stage where most of my clients disclose. The precipitating event is usually negative feedback from a supervisor, conflict with a co-worker, disciplinary action, placement on a PIP, or being given two week's notice to improve (which is almost always means termination is imminent). Disclosure compels the employer to try to make reasonable accommodations, and gives the individual time to seek professional services if needed.

Avoid when: there are no performance problems or need for accommodation.

TIPS AND ADVICE
The Need May Not Be for Accommodation
Several years ago, I was contacted by a man who cleaned rooms at a hotel. He wanted to disclose his Asperger's Syndrome to his boss. "She yells at me all the time," he said, "because I am too slow. I've told her that I can't work as fast as the others, or clean as many rooms a day."

This man was not able to meet a clearly stated productivity requirement. The need was not for accommodation; he needed to find a different job.

I have also had cases where relationships between my client and his employer have deteriorated to the point where there is no hope of reconciliation. These situations create an enormous amount of stress. Each side becomes preoccupied with documenting errors, performance shortfalls, breaches of conduct or possible violations of the law. It is not possible to accommodate such situations. Unless an individual can transfer to a different part of the organization, I encourage him to seek other employment.

Accommodations and basic job readiness skills should not be confused. Asking an employer to adjust a work schedule, because an individual has trouble managing his time, is a job readiness issue. Asking for an adjustment because the individual has to attend medical appointments is an accommodation.

In most workplaces, there is zero tolerance for any behavior that can be construed as a threat or harassment. The ADA states that employers do not have to accommodate employees who pose a direct threat to the health or safety of themselves or others, or those who engage in serious misconduct. Losing your temper at work can be considered a direct threat. It is not reasonable to expect that an organization will or should tolerate explosive outbursts. Employees who cannot control these emotions need to seek the services of a professional.

The Need May Not Be for Disclosure

It may be possible to address problems without disclosing a disability. Explanatory statements may be enough to "neutralize" unexpected behaviors and smooth over misunderstandings. Some of my clients have had success by explaining that they are hyper-sensitive to noise, have poor memory or tend to look angry when they are concentrating.

The Release of Medical Information Should Be Controlled

Typically, employees are given a form for their medical provider to fill out after they disclose. It asks for proof of diagnosis and an explanation of how the disability impacts work performance. Individuals can and should control what information is given to an employer. It is not necessary or desirable to submit a full neuropsychological evaluation or an entire medical history. If you are a clinician, focus on information that impacts the individual *in his current job*. It is acceptable for other service providers who are working with the individual to submit accommodation recommendations.

Many Accommodations Are No or Low Cost

I do not assume that accommodating an individual will be costly to an employer. Often, the opposite is true. Here are examples of workplace accommodations that my clients have asked for and been granted:

- use of laptop for note-taking during meetings

- meeting notes taken by a colleague

- weekly meetings with supervisor to clarify expectations and identify priorities

- written instructions for tasks and procedures

- lobby television turned off during shift (for a receptionist)

- non-essential scheduling tasks reassigned to a co-worker

- permission to take breaks when stressed

- requests from staff members submitted in writing

- interview questions submitted in advance

- switch to a technical job from a management role

- move to a quiet workspace

- use of headphones to block out noise.

If the individual is working with a coach, speech–language pathologist or other professional to address difficulties, this should be communicated to an employer. It demonstrates the employee's commitment to being successful on the job. Some companies will reimburse employees for outside coaching. The supervisor of one man I coached was so happy with his progress that she made a special arrangement for the company to reimburse him for the coaching.

Worksheet 8.1 is a rating scale that I use to help a client determine whether it is in his interest to disclose.

Worksheet 8.1

DISCLOSURE NEED AND ACTION SCALE

How Serious Is the Problem?	Possible Action Steps
Level 3: Immediate Action Required ☐ Formal disciplinary action; probation or two weeks' notice to improve ☐ Formal meeting with supervisor about performance problems; written warning; placed on Performance Improvement Plan	☐ Disclosure and formal accommodation request ☐ Engage a professional to intervene on my behalf ☐ Other:
Level 2: Corrective Action Needed ☐ Same performance problem has been mentioned more than twice ☐ I am consistently re-doing assignments ☐ Assignments are late on a regular basis	☐ Disclosure and formal accommodation request ☐ Talk to supervisor about difficulties; suggest solutions without formal disclosure ☐ Ask a co-worker for ideas about improving performance ☐ Evaluate whether this is the right job or career ☐ Other:
Level 1: Needs My Attention ☐ Working very long hours ☐ Confused about what is expected ☐ Continually re-checking work; forgetting steps ☐ Told that I am asking too many questions/should know what to do by now ☐ Anxious and unsure about performance	☐ Ask a co-worker for ideas on improving performance ☐ Meet regularly with supervisor to clarify priorities and expectations ☐ Use check lists; make notes Request additional training ☐ Find ways to manage stress and anxiety ☐ Other:

FINAL THOUGHTS

Coaching individuals with Asperger's Syndrome is the hardest work that I have ever done. It is also the most rewarding. A decade ago, I never would have imagined that one day I'd be focused on pragmatics and executive function rather than marketing strategies and sales forecasts. I am very grateful to have found a second career that is interesting, challenging, and that enables me to be of service to others. This work is also humbling. The majority of people with Asperger's Syndrome struggle to find and sustain employment.

I believe that things are beginning to change, because the number of people identified as being on the autism spectrum is so large. There are more and more resources to assist career counselors at colleges and universities, and vocational rehabilitation specialists, who work with these individuals. The organizations that I mentioned in Chapter 3, and others like them, are creating jobs that are manageable and pay a living wage. Additionally, the positive publicity they generate inspires others to take action in their communities.

Recently, I have received an increased number of inquiries from employers. They are interested in assisting employees who have disclosed Asperger's Syndrome, and in training for their human resources and hiring managers. This suggests to me that greater numbers of companies are recognizing that people on the autism spectrum represent a skilled labor force.

Whether you are a parent, professional or business person, I hope that this book has given you new insight into adults at work. I have been fortunate to coach a diverse cross section of individuals. My intention has been to share stories, including some that are humorous, that show how real people cope with real situations. For all of their differences, people with Asperger's Syndrome want the same things that neurotypicals do: independence, a place within the community and the chance to contribute their skills in a meaningful way.

I wish that I could say that every client has found the job of his dreams. Or tell you about a secret system I discovered that removes all of the barriers. Unfortunately, there is no magic or easy answer. Most of my clients make marked progress toward their goals. For some, the coaching progresses in an orderly way. Career options are explored, interview skills are practiced, performance problems addressed and accommodations decided. In a few weeks, the work is done. With others, the coaching relationship is longer and more intense. Over the course of months, or even years, I come to know these individuals quite well. I am intimately acquainted with bosses, co-workers and other important people and events in their lives. I follow along as various challenges are encountered and solved.

This is the best of times and the worst of times. We still talk about "tsunamis" of autistic young people who are coming of age and unable to find jobs. "Crisis" is used to describe the employment situation for those on the spectrum. However, the understanding and appreciation of these individuals is also increasing. Parents, professionals and business leaders are asking "what if," and creating opportunities for all to benefit from the talents of Aspergians and others on the spectrum.

I hope that in some small way this book will contribute to those efforts, so that people with Asperger's Syndrome will be able to use their skills to their, and our, benefit.

REFERENCES

American Medical Association (2014)"ICD-10 Code Set to Replace ICD-9." http://www.ama-assn.org/ama/pub/physician-resources/solutions-managing-your-practice/coding-billing-insurance/hipaahealth-insurance-portability-accountability-act/transaction-code-set-standards/icd10-code-set.page, accessed on 27 September, 2014.

American Psychiatric Association (APA) (2013) *Diagnostic and Statistical Manual of Mental Disorders, Fifth Edition*. Arlington, VA: American Psychiatric Association.

Attwood, T. (2007) *The Complete Guide to Asperger's Syndrome*. London and Philadelphia, PA: Jessica Kingsley Publishers.

Barkley, R. (2011) *Barkley Deficits in Executive Functioning Scale (BDEFS)*. New York: The Guilford Press.

Baron-Cohen, S. (2011) "Simon-Baron Cohen Replies to Rachel Cohen-Rottenberg." Autism Blogs Directory. Available at http://autismblogsdirectory.blogspot.com/2011/09/simon-baron-cohen-replies-to-rachel.html, accessed on June 23, 2014.

Berger, J.G and Fitzgerald, C. (2002) *Executive Coaching, Practices and perspectives*. Mountain View, CA: Davies-Black Publishing.

Briers, S. (2012) *Brilliant Cognitive Behavioural Therapy*, 2nd edn. Harlow: Pearson Education.

Burns, D. (1999) *Feeling Good, The New Mood Therapy*. New York: HarperCollins.

Centers for Disease Control and Prevention (2014) "CDC estimates 1 in 68 children has been identified with autism spectrum disorder." Press Release. Available at www.cdc.gov/media/releases/2014/p0327-autism-spectrum-disorder.html, accessed on June 24, 2014.

Cherry, K. (2013) "The Milgram Obedience Experiment, the Perils of Obedience." About.com. Available at http://psychology.about.com/od/historyofpsychology/a/milgram.htm, accessed on June 24, 2014.

Cherry, K. (2014a) "What is Top-Down Processing?" About.com. Available at http://psychology.about.com/od/tindex/g/top-down-processing.htm, accessed June 24, 2014.

Cherry, K. (2014b) "What Is Problem-Solving?" About.com. Available at http://psychology.about.com/od/problemsolving/f/problem-solving-steps.htm, accessed on June 24, 2014.

Cohen, M.R. (2011) *Social Literacy, A Social Skills Seminar for Young Adults with ASDs, NLDs, and Social Anxiety*. Baltimore, MD: Paul H. Brooks Publishing.

De Haan, E. (2006) "Coaching and Mentoring: Three Millennia of One-to-One Learning," *Coach & Mentor*, Spring. Available at: www.ashridge.org.uk/website/IC.nsf/wFARATT/Coaching+and+Mentoring:+three+millennia+of+one-to-one+learning?OpenDocument, accessed on June 24, 2014.

Dingfelder, S. (2006) "Postgrad Growth Area: Executive Coaching." *gradPSYCH* magazine, American Psychological Association. Available at www.apa.org/gradpsych/2006/11/coaching.aspx, accessed on June 24, 2014.

Eikleberry, C. (2007) *The Career Guide for Creative and Unconventional People*, 3rd edn. New York: Ten Speed Press.

ePredix (1999) *Successful Executive's Handbook, Development Suggestions for Today's Executives.* Minneapolis, MN: EPredix and Personnel Decisions International.

Equip for Equality (2005) "The ADA and Personality Testing by Employers, Karracker v. Rent-A-Center." Fact Sheet. Available at www.equipforequality.org/?s=MMPI+and+Rent+a+Center, accessed on June 24, 2014.

Fast, Y. (2004) *Employment for Individuals with Asperger Syndrome or Non-Verbal Learning Disability.* London and Philadelphia, PA: Jessica Kingsley Publishers.

Fein, D. (ed.) (2011) *The Neuropsychology of Autism*. New York: Oxford University Press.

Finch, D. (2012) *The Journal of Best Practices, A Memoir of Marriage, Asperger Syndrome, and One Man's Quest to Be a Better Husband*. New York: Scribner.

Fogle, P.T. (2013) *Essentials of Communication Sciences and Disorders*. Clifton Park, NY: Cengage Learning Inc.

Frith, U. (2003) *Autism, Explaining the Enigma*, 2nd edn. Malden, MA: Blackwell Publishing.

Frith, U. (2008) *Autism, A Very Short Introduction*. New York: Oxford University Press, Inc.

Fritscher, L. (2014) "Information Processing." Available at http://phobias.about.com/od/glossary/g/Information-Processing.htm About.com, accessed on June 24, 2014.

Gabor, D. (2001) *How to Start a Conversation and Make Friends*. New York: Fireside.

Gathercole, S.E. and Alloway, T.P. (2008) *Working Memory & Learning*. London: Sage Publications.

Gaus, V. (2007) *Cognitive-Behavioral Therapy for Adult Asperger Syndrome*. New York: Guilford Press.

Gaus, V. (2011) *Living Well on the Spectrum*. New York: Guilford Press.

Goleman, D. (1998) *Working with Emotional Intelligence*. New York: Bantam Books.

Grandin, T. (2006) *Thinking in Pictures, My Life with Autism*. New York: Vintage Books.

International Coach Federation (2012) "2012 ICF Global Coaching Study, Data Appendix." Available at http://icf.files.cms-plus.com/includes/media/docs/ICF-Region-NORTH-AMERICA.pdf, accessed on June 24, 2014.

Job Accommodation Network (2010) "Accommodation and Compliance Series, Testing Accommodations." Available at http://askjan.org/media/downloads/TestingAccomm.pdf, accessed on June 24, 2014.

Leonard, T. (n.d.) "About Thomas Leonard." Available at http://thomasleonardphotos.wordpress.com/about/, accessed on June 24, 2014.

Leonard, T. (2003) "Thomas Leonard Bio." Available at www.thomasleonard.com/bio.html. Accessed on June 24, 2014.

Lewis, M. (2011) *TheBig Short: Inside the Doomsday Machine*. New York: W.W. Norton & Company

Mamen, M. (2007) *Understanding Nonverbal Learning Disabilities*. London and Philadelphia, PA: Jessica Kingsley Publishers.

McLeod, S. (2007) "Psychodynamic Approach." Available at www.simplypsychology.org/psychodynamic.html, accessed on June 24, 2014.

Mehrabian, A. (1981) *Silent Messages: Implicit Communication of Emotions and Attitudes*. Belmont, CA: Wadsworth (currently being distributed by Albert Mehrabian, am@kaaj.com).

Meltzer, L. (2010) *Promoting Executive Function in the Classroom*. New York: Guilford Press.

Mottron, L. (2011) "Changing Perceptions: The Power of Autism." *Nature 479*, 33–35.

Myles, B.S., Tapscott Cook, K., Miller, N.E., Rinner, L. and Robbins, L.A. (2000) *Asperger Syndrome and Sensory Issues, Practical Solutions for Making Sense of the World.* Shawnee Mission, KS: Autism Asperger Publishing Company.

Peltier, B. (2001) *The Psychology of Executive Coaching, Theory and Application.* New York: Brunner-Routledge.

Previsor and Personnel Decisions (2010) *Successful Manager's Handbook,* 8th edn. Roswell, GA: PreVisor Inc. and Minneapolis, MN: Personnel Decisions International.

Rock, D. (2006) *Quiet Leadership.* New York: HarperCollins.

Skedgell, K.E. (2012) "History of the Coach." Writer of Historical and the Fantastic, blog. Available at http://keskedgell.blogspot.com/2012/07/history-of-coach.html, accessed on June 24, 2014.

Standifer, W.S. (2011) "Fact Sheet on Autism Employment." University of Missouri, Disability Policy & Studies. Available at http://dps.missouri.edu/Autism/AutismFactSheet2011.pdf, accessed on June 24, 2014.

Stettner, M. (2000) *Skills for New Managers.* Madison, WI: McGraw-Hill.

Thompson, S. (1997) *The Source® for Nonverbal Learning Disorders.* East Moline, IL: LinguiSystem, Inc.

Vermeulen, P. (2012) *Autism as Context Blindness.* Shawnee Mission, KS: Autism Asperger Publishing Company.

Winner, M.G. (2005) *Worksheets! for Teaching Social Thinking and Related Skills.* San Jose, CA: Michelle Garcia Winner, SLP.

Winner, M.G. and Crooke, P. (2011) *Social Thinking at Work, Why Should I Care?* San Jose, CA: Think Social Publishing Inc.

INDEX